COUNTRIES OF THE WORLD

Bolivia

Gareth Stevens Publishing
A WORLD ALMANAC EDUCATION GROUP COMPANY

About the Authors: Leticia Gómez was born in Texas and raised in New Mexico. For three years she was the associate publisher and editor of *El Voceador*, a bilingual English–Spanish newspaper. She has also worked as a journalist, technical writer, and columnist.

A graduate of Oxford and London universities, Paul A. Rozario is a professional writer and editor of reference books for young readers. His list of book credits includes titles on African and American indigenous peoples and cultures, festivals, and the environment.

PICTURE CREDITS

Written by
LETICIA GÓMEZ
PAUL A. ROZARIO

Edited by
YUMI NG
PAUL A. ROZARIO

Edited in the U.S. by
JONATHA A. BROWN
MARY DYKSTRA
ALAN WACHTEL

Designed by
BENSON TAN

Picture research by
SUSAN JANE MANUEL
THOMAS KHOO

First published in North America in 2004 by
Gareth Stevens Publishing
A World Almanac Education Group Company
330 West Olive Street, Suite 100
Milwaukee, Wisconsin 53212 USA

Please visit our web site at
www.garethstevens.com
For a free color catalog describing
Gareth Stevens Publishing's list of high-quality
books and multimedia programs, call
1-800-542-2595 (USA) or 1-800-387-3178 (Canada)
Gareth Stevens Publishing's fax: (414) 332-3567.

© **TIMES MEDIA PRIVATE LIMITED 2004**
Originated and designed by
Times Editions
An imprint of Times Media Private Limited
A member of the Times Publishing Group
Times Centre, 1 New Industrial Road
Singapore 536196
http://www.timesone.com.sg/te

Library of Congress Cataloging-in-Publication Data
Gómez, Leticia, 1966–
Bolivia / Leticia Gómez and Paul Rozario.
p. cm. — (Countries of the world)
Summary: An overview of Bolivia that includes information on geography, history, government, language, culture, and relations with North America.
Includes bibliographical references and index.
ISBN 0-8368-3108-X (lib. bdg.)
1. Bolivia—Juvenile literature. [1. Bolivia.]
I. Rozario, Paul. II. Title. III. Countries of the world (Milwaukee, Wis.)
F3308.5.G66   2004
984—dc22   2003060382

Printed in Singapore

1 2 3 4 5 6 7 8 9 08 07 06 05 04

Contents

AN OVERVIEW OF BOLIVIA

The Republic of Bolivia is named after Simón Bolívar, a hero of South America's independence. Long before the time of Bolívar, the land that became Bolivia had an illustrious past. The ancient Tiwanaku Empire developed near Lake Titicaca, leaving behind exquisite temples and art objects. Ruins of the great Inca Empire are also found in Bolivia. Spanish colonial rule has also left behind a legacy of beautiful art and architecture. Despite having a rich history and awe inspiring natural beauty, Bolivia remains a poorly known country, but it is working hard to improve socioeconomic conditions and build a better life for its people

Opposite: **A Bolivian woman buys fresh produce at an outdoor market in Potosí.**

Below: **Bolivian children pose in front of their school in Yacuces, Santa Cruz.**

THE FLAG OF BOLIVIA

The flag of Bolivia, adopted in 1851, is divided into three equal horizontal bands. The top band's red stands for the blood shed by Bolivia's war heroes. The yellow band in the center represents the country's mineral wealth, while the green band at the bottom points to Bolivia's rich flora. The coat of arms rests at the center of the yellow band. The oval inside features the word "Bolivia," with ten stars adorning the lower half. Inside the oval, images of the Potosí Mountain, a breadfruit tree, a sheaf of wheat, and a llama complete the shield. A bird is perched atop the coat of arms.

Geography

Bolivia is a landlocked country with an area of 424,164 square miles (1,098,581 square kilometers). It borders Brazil to the north and east, Paraguay to the southeast, Argentina to the south, Chile to the southwest and west, and Peru to the northwest.

Rugged Western Highlands

Western Bolivia is an extremely mountainous region. The peaks there form part of the Andes Mountains, stretching from the northern coast of South America to the southern end of the continent. Two nearly parallel mountain chains dominate western Bolivia: the Cordillera Occidental, which runs along the country's western border with Chile, and the Cordillera Oriental, which runs roughly northwest to southeast, close to the central part of Bolivia. The Cordillera Occidental is home to Bolivia's highest peak, Mount Sajama, which rises 21,463 feet (6,542 meters) above sea level, near the country's border with Chile and Peru. The northern portion of the Cordillera Oriental is called the Cordillera Real and is more than 200 miles (320 km) long.

ILLIMANI AND HUAYNA POTOSÍ

These two mountains near La Paz are favorite spots for Bolivian and foreign trekkers.
(A Closer Look, page 54)

Below: During the dry season, the Andes Mountains in Bolivia are bare of vegetation, except for the hardy ichu plant, which is eaten by llamas.

The Altiplano, a highland region situated at an average elevation of about 12,000 feet (3,650 m) above sea level, lies between the Cordillera Occidental and the Cordillera Oriental. The Altiplano stretches from southern Peru to southwestern Bolivia, a distance of about 600 miles (965 km).

Above: **Lake Chalviri in Oruro lies high in the Bolivian Andes.**

Lowland Plains, Swamps, and Jungles

East of the cordilleras, the land is much lower. From snowcapped heights, the terrain quickly descends into a region of thick rain forests called the Yungas. From there, the land slopes downward to reach low plains, open savannas, tropical forests, extensive swamps, and jungles. This is the Oriente region of Bolivia, which occupies more than two-thirds of the country.

Rivers and Lakes

Major rivers in Bolivia include the Beni, Mamoré, and Iténez Rivers in the north, the last forming the border between Bolivia and Brazil. The Pilcomayo River in the south of the country forms part of the border with Argentina. Important Bolivian lakes include Lake Titicaca on the Altiplano and Lakes Rogagua and Rogoaguado in the north of the country.

UYUNI SALT FLAT

The Uyuni Salt Flat is a huge salt desert that extends over the southwestern part of the Bolivian Altiplano.
(A Closer Look, page 72)

LAKE TITICACA

The world's highest navigable lake, Lake Titicaca was a sacred place for the Incas.
(A Closer Look, page 58)

Climate

In Bolivia, temperature and climate are determined not only by the time of the year, but also by location and elevation. In the Bolivian Andes, the rainy season falls between December and March, with rainfall varying considerably according to elevation. During the day, temperatures can rise as high as 60° Fahrenheit (16° Celsius), but the average temperature usually falls between 45° F and 52° F (7° C and 11° C). Nighttime temperatures are much lower and can fall below freezing in winter. Near Lake Titicaca, temperatures are more moderate, however, with daytime temperatures climbing as high as 70° F (21° C). On the Altiplano, cold winds blow year-round.

In the Oriente region, the climate is hot. Temperatures in the north average up to 80° F (27° C), while those in the south range between 73° F and 77° F (23° C and 25° C). The forests of the Yungas, which lie between the highlands and the lowlands, are cool and humid, with temperatures ranging from 60° F to 68° F (16° C to 20° C)

Below: Viscachas scurry among rocks on Fisherman's Island in Potosí's Uyuni Salt Flat.

Left: The llama is used as a beast of burden by the people of the Bolivian Andes, as well as by other highland communities in Peru, Ecuador, Chile, and Argentina. An average llama measures about 47 inches (120 cm) at the shoulder and can carry a load of between 100 and 132 pounds (45 and 60 kilograms) about 15 to 20 miles (25 to 30 km) in a day. The animal also provides food, in the form of meat, and wool and hides for clothes, rope, and rugs. The dried dung of the llama provides fuel when burned.

Plants and Animals

Bolivia supports a huge diversity of plant and animal species. Although the southern reaches of the Altiplano are too salty for plant life, the northern regions support wild grasses and shrubs such as ichu, tola, yareta, and cactus shrub. Totora reeds, eucalyptus, and pine trees grow on the banks of Lake Titicaca, while indigenous tree species such as quishuara and khena are found in other areas. Much of the Altiplano has been turned into farmland for potato, quinoa, barley, wheat, and fava bean crops. Animal species on the Altiplano include the llama, vicuña, alpaca, and guanaco, which are all members of the camel family, as well as the Andean condor, the largest bird in the Americas.

The forests of the Yungas valleys are home to a large variety of tropical hardwood trees, medicinal plants, and fruit trees. Green pine, laurel, cedar, and coffee all thrive at this altitude. Vegetation in the lowlands includes tropical rain forests in the northern Oriente and scrub in the southern region of Chaco. The northern forests support mammal species such as the jaguar, sloth, tapir, and monkeys. Rivers teem with frogs, caimans, and many fish species, including the piranha. The plains and savannas are home to species such as the armadillo, wild pig, puma, and marsh deer, as well as the capybara, the largest rodent in the world.

DINOSAUR FOOTPRINTS

Cal Orcko, near Sucre in central Bolivia, is home to the world's largest collection of dinosaur tracks.
(*A Closer Look,* page 50)

NATIONAL PARKS AND OTHER PROTECTED AREAS

Bolivia's national parks and protected areas help conserve the nation's rich biological heritage.
(*A Closer Look,* page 60)

History

Archaeologists have uncovered human bones in the Andes that are between 10,000 and 12,000 years old, but they believe that human settlement of the area took place much earlier.

The Tiwanaku Empire

Bolivia's history originates in ancient American cultures that are known as pre-Columbian civilizations. One of these, the Tiwanaku Empire, established itself on the southern shores of Lake Titicaca on the Altiplano between 200 and 600 A.D. An advanced people, the Tiwanaku used a unique agricultural irrigation system that helped prevent crops from freezing during cold Altiplano nights. Using raised terraces surrounded by small canals of water, farmers were able to regulate the temperature of their fields. Remains of this irrigation system can still be seen today, along with those of such remarkable Tiwanaku monuments as the Kalasasaya, which features tall columns carved out of stone and carvings of religious figures, and the Akapana Pyramid.

TIWANAKU CIVILIZATION

The ancient Tiwanaku civilization was centered on the Bolivian Altiplano.
(A Closer Look, page 68)

ATLANTIS IN BOLIVIA

Some explorers believe the lost city of Atlantis is located in Bolivia.
(A Closer Look, page 44)

Below: **This golden mask dates from before the tenth century A.D. and depicts an Inca and Tiwanaku deity.**

Under Inca and Spanish Rule

The Tiwanaku civilization disappeared by 1200 A.D. and was replaced by smaller kingdoms. These cultures, in turn, became part of the expanding and Quechua-speaking Inca civilization, which had its base in Cuzco, Peru. The Incan rulers sent many Quechua speakers to live among the Aymara communities of the Bolivian highlands, thereby giving modern Bolivia its unique mix of indigenous Indian groups.

Bolivia's Aymara and Quechua peoples suffered greatly under Spanish rule, which began in the sixteenth century. Many Bolivians were sent to work in silver mines that had been opened by the Spanish conquistadores. Hundreds of thousands of Bolivians are believed to have died from the difficult conditions of the silver mines. Important Bolivian cities were also founded during this period, including Sucre in 1538, Potosí in 1545, La Paz in 1548, Cochabamba in 1571, and Oruro in 1608. Together, these cities made up Upper Peru, the most densely populated and richest of Spain's American possessions, from the sixteenth to the eighteenth centuries. In the early 1800s, many South American cities, including La Paz and Sucre, began rebelling against Spanish rule, and Bolivia became an independent country on August 6, 1825.

Above: This stone relief in Plaza Murillo in La Paz depicts the arrival of Spanish soldiers in South America.

INDEPENDENCE

In the early 1800s, Napoleon invaded Spain and placed a French king in control. People in the Spanish colonies began to protest the colonial government set up by the French king, but revolts in Bolivia were quickly squelched in 1809. These protests and revolts formed the beginning of the independence movement. Leaders such as Simón Bolívar and Antonio José de Sucre Alcalá led South American armies against the Spaniards.

11

Early Decrees of the Republic

The early decades of the Bolivian republic were characterized by economic decline. Revenues from silver mining fell sharply and some ten thousand mines were abandoned by 1846. Bolivia's economy quickly fell behind those of neighbors such as Chile, which began to grow rich from grain and meat production. Although rich in natural resources such as nitrate minerals, the country lacked the ability to exploit these resources, choosing instead to mine the remaining silver deposits on the Altiplano.

The War of the Pacific (1879–1883)

In the 1840s, Chilean companies began mining nitrates in Bolivia. Later, more nitrate deposits were found deeper within Bolivian territory, and a dispute between Chile and Bolivia arose over taxes levied by Bolivian authorities on the export of the Chilean-mined nitrates. In 1878, the Bolivian government tried to increase this export tax. Chile retaliated by occupying the Bolivian port of Antofagasta and the surrounding areas in February 1879. Bolivian and Peruvian forces tried to rout the Chileans in various battles over the next year, but failed. The 1884 truce between Chile and Bolivia resulted in Bolivia losing territory, including access to the Pacific Ocean.

SIMÓN BOLÍVAR
The Liberator Simón Bolívar was born in Caracas, Venezuela, but five South American nations owe their liberty to him: Bolivia, Colombia, Ecuador, Peru, and Venezuela.
(A Closer Look, page 48)

Left: **Fishermen collect the day's catch at the port of Antofagasta, Chile. Bolivia lost this port, along with its entire seacoast, to Chile in the War of the Pacific.**

Left: **Representatives from the governments of Argentina and Bolivia sign a peace treaty in Buenos Aires in July 1938 to end the Chaco War between Bolivia and Paraguay.**

Into the Twentieth Century

The decades following Bolivia's loss of its Pacific coast were marked by political and economic stability. A series of civilian governments came to power, and the country's political parties united to promote the mining industry and strengthen Bolivia's economy. Improving the country's internal communication and transportation systems was also a priority for the authorities. By 1920, a railway network linked most of Bolivia's main cities. Train service also connected La Paz to the Chilean Pacific ports of Antofagasta and Arica.

From 1932 to 1935, Bolivia fought a war with Paraguay over the Chaco Boreal region in southeastern Bolivia. The Chaco War ended with Bolivia losing territory to Paraguay. Between 1936 and 1952, Bolivia was ruled by many governments, both civilian and military. Different political parties were active during this period, including the Movimento Nacionalista Revolucionario, or MNR, and the Partido de la Izquierda Revolucionaria, or PIR.

In 1952, the MNR came to power in Bolivia and initiated major social reforms. Bolivia's Indian population was given the right to vote, as well as the right to own land. The MNR stayed in power until 1964, when Bolivia came to be ruled by the first in a series of military governments. The political situation became especially unstable between 1978 and 1982, during which time Bolivia had ten different governments, both civilian and military.

SILVER MINES OF POTOSÍ

The silver mines of Potosí provided the Spanish Empire with great wealth during the sixteenth and seventeenth centuries. Hundreds of thousands of Indian and African slaves died in the mines *(A Closer Look, page 70)*

13

Moving towards Democracy, Improving the Economy

In 1982, Bolivia returned to a democratic government. The 1980s were a period of economic turmoil for the country. By 1985, inflation was at an all-time high, and banks and industries were on the verge of shutting down. The agriculture sector was also failing because of unusual weather patterns associated with the El Niño effect. The newly appointed government attempted to solve these problems with economic reforms that included devaluing the currency, closing down industrial sectors that were doing badly, and implementing a wage freeze for workers. These changes helped Bolivia bring down the country's high rate of inflation and improve the economy.

In 1993, the owner of Bolivia's largest mining company, Gonzalo Sánchez de Lozada Bustamente, became president of the country. He privatized many companies, including those in the energy, transportation, and petrochemical industries. This move brought foreign investments to Bolivia. In 1997, Sánchez de Lozada was succeeded by Hugo Bánzer Suárez, but was reelected president in 2002. Sánchez de Lozada promised to tackle Bolivia's social and economic problems. Currently, the main opposition politician is Evo Morales, an Aymara who has the strong support of Bolivia's Indian communities.

HUGO BÁNZER SUÁREZ (1926–2002)

General Hugo Bánzer Suárez was born on May 10, 1926, in Concepcíon. He was the grandson of German immigrants and son of an army officer. Bánzer trained as a soldier at the U.S. Army's School of the Americas in Panama and Fort Hood, Texas. In 1971, Bánzer toppled General Juan José Torres and established a long and brutal regime, which is believed to be responsible for dozens of disappearances and at least 200 deaths. Due to pressure from within Bolivia and from the United States, Bánzer called for an election in 1978. He was then forced out of office. In 1997, as the head of a seven-party coalition, Bánzer took office as a civilian. Due to poor health, Bánzer resigned in August 2001. He died in May 2002.

Left: General Hugo Bánzer Suárez twice served as president of Bolivia.

Antonio José de Sucre Alcalá (1795–1830)

General Antonio Jóse de Sucre Alcalá was born in Cumaná, Venezuela. He served as Simón Bolívar's general during Bolívar's military campaign to rid South America of Spanish rule. Sucre liberated Ecuador in 1822. In 1824, Sucre's armies won the Battle of Ayacucho, which led to Peru's independence from Spain. A year later, Sucre took control of Bolivia from the Spanish. He became Bolivia's first president in 1826 and tried to institute social and economic reforms. However, he was forced to resign due to strong opposition to his policies. Sucre left Bolivia in 1828 for Quito, Ecuador, and died two years later, the victim of an assassination.

Antonio Jóse
de Sucre Alcalá

Víctor Paz Estenssoro (1907–2001)

Víctor Paz Estenssoro is one of the most important political figures in Bolivian history. Born in Tarija, he was an economist by profession. In 1941, he and others formed the political party Movimento Nacionalista Revolucionario (MNR). Paz Estenssoro was elected president of Bolivia in 1952 and began a far-reaching program of social and economic reforms. Between 1956 and 1960, he served as Bolivia's ambassador to the United Kingdom. Reelected president in 1960, Paz Estenssoro then reorganized Bolivia's tin industry with the help of foreign economic advisors. He served Bolivia as president for a third time between 1985 and 1989, during which he implemented policies to reduce inflation. Paz Estenssoro died on June 7, 2001.

Víctor Paz Estenssoro

Lidia Gueiler Tejada (1921–)

Lidia Gueiler Tejada was the first woman president of Bolivia. Her previous appointments included serving as a member of parliament between 1956 and 1964, undersecretary for agriculture, and head of the Chamber of Deputies. The Bolivian congress appointed Gueiler Tejada president in November 1979 to govern until elections were held in June of the following year. Soon after the 1980 elections, however, a military coup led by General Luis García Meza toppled her government. During the 1980s, Gueiler Tejada went into exile briefly in France. She later served as Bolivia's ambassador to the former West Germany, and, later, to Venezuela.

Lidia Gueiler Tejada

Government and the Economy

Bolivia is a democratic republic and has a government divided into three branches: executive, legislative, and judiciary.

The executive branch consists of the president, the vice president, and a cabinet of ministers. Both the president and the vice president are elected to five-year terms and cannot be reelected to successive second terms. The cabinet consists of the heads of the various ministries of state, who are appointed by the president.

The National Congress forms the legislative arm of the government and is made up two houses: the Chamber of Senators and the Chamber of Deputies. Twenty-seven senators sit in the Chamber of Senators, while the Chamber of Deputies consists of 127 members. Both senators and deputies are elected to five-year terms.

Bolivia's judiciary branch is made up of the Supreme Court, a Constitutional Tribunal, and district, provincial, and local courts. Twelve judges sit on the Supreme Court, while five judges

PRIVATIZATION OF WATER IN COCHABAMBA

In 1999, the Bolivian government decided to sell off the water supply of the city of Cochabamba to a private international corporation. When the new water company announced its plans to raise the water rates, the citizens of Cochabamba, led by a grassroots leader, took to the streets in protest. The government eventually agreed to reverse the privatization measure, and the people were allowed to have direct control over their water supply.
(*A Closer Look, page 64*)

BOLIVIA'S CONSTITUTION

Bolivia's first constitution dates from 1826. The current constitution, enacted in 1994, is a revision of the 1967 constitution and was further amended in 1995.

Left: An Amerindian woman casts her vote at the mayoral election in Coripata, a town in the Yungas of La Paz, in December 1999.

preside over the Constitutional Tribunal. The Constitutional Tribunal determines whether or not laws are enacted according to the Bolivian constitution and also helps resolve disputes between different government branches and agencies. The district, provincial, and local courts try minor cases. Appointed by the National Congress, the judges of the Supreme Court and the Constitutional Tribunal serve ten-year terms.

Above: **The National Congress building in La Paz first housed a convent and then a university, before it was given its present use in 1904.**

Local Government

Bolivia's local administration is divided into nine geographic *departamentos*, or departments: Beni, Chuquisaca, Cochabamba, La Paz, Oruro, Pando, Potosí, Santa Cruz, and Tarija. Each department is run by a prefect. The departments elect councils that control revenue and expenditures. Each department also elects three senators to represent the department in the Chamber of Senators. Departments are divided into provinces, which are in turn subdivided into municipalities. Each municipality is divided into cantons. In 2002, there were 112 provinces, 312 municipalities, and 1,384 cantons.

POLITICAL PARTIES

Major political parties in Bolivia include Movimiento Nacionalista Revolucionario (MNR), Movimiento de la Izquierda Revolucionaria (MIR), and Movimiento al Socialismo (MAS). In the 2002 elections, MNR won forty-seven seats in the National Congress, making it the political party with the largest number of seats in the Bolivian legislature.

A Changing Economy

Bolivia is rich in natural resources, including minerals, petroleum and natural gas, and forests. In fact, Bolivia has the second largest reserves of natural gas in South America. The country, however, has been slow to exploit this natural wealth mainly due to the lack of new investment, high costs of production, and poor transportation, including no direct access to the sea. Bolivia, therefore, has had to depend on subsistence agriculture and the mining of silver and tin. The prices of these minerals have fluctuated widely in the past, devastating Bolivia's economy on more than one occasion.

In the late twentieth century, the Bolivian economy was dramatically reformed. One major reform was the privatization of many companies previously owned by the government. This move generated billions of dollars in new economic investment and contributed to overall economic growth. The economy is also set to benefit from the further development of the oil and natural gas industry, improvements to the agricultural and mining sectors, and investments in the hydroelectric power and water industries.

TRADE

Boliva's major exports in 2000 were soybeans, natural gas, zinc, gold, and wood. Total exports in 2002 were estimated to be about U.S. $1.3 billion. Imports in 2002 included raw materials, chemicals, petroleum, and food and totaled an estimated U.S. $1.6 billion. The country's major trading partners in 2001 include Brazil, the United States, and Argentina.

Below: **The majority of Bolivians work in small-scale agriculture. Farmers sell their produce at Bolivia's many markets, like this one in Santa Cruz.**

Agriculture

Agriculture employs about two-fifths of the country's working population and contributed an estimated 20 percent of Bolivia's gross domestic product (GDP) in 2002. Crops cultivated on the Altiplano include the potato (available in numerous varieties); the oca, another kind of tuber; grains, such as quinoa, cañahua, barley, wheat, and corn; and fava beans. Farmers in the Yungas grow coffee, cacao, sweet potatoes, cassava, and chili peppers, as well as a host of fruits such as oranges, bananas, avocados, pineapples, mangoes, papayas, and melons. The coca leaf is also grown in the Yungas. Soybeans are the main crop grown around the city of Santa Cruz in the Oriente region and have become one of the most important of Bolivia's exports.

Mining

In 2000, Bolivia's mining sector contributed 11.7 percent of the country's gross domestic product but only employed a small percentage of the working population. Traditionally, silver and tin have been Bolivia's main mineral exports. At the end of the twentieth century, however, gold was fast becoming a major export. Bolivia's tin-mining industry faces stiff competition from other tin-producing nations, including Malaysia, Indonesia, and Thailand. The country also has deposits of zinc, lead, and iron ore that can be mined in potentially lucrative quantities.

COCA LEAVES

Bolivia is one of the world's largest producers of coca leaves. The wild coca plant has been harvested in the Andes since the time of the Incan Empire and was used by the Incas during special ceremonies. A tea made from coca leaves helps cure altitude sickness, while for hundreds of years Bolivian miners have chewed coca leaves to gain the strength to work in the mines. Most of the coca leaves grown today, however, are used to produce cocaine, an illegal drug. Many poor Bolivian farmers, who have had no other means to make a living, harvest coca to survive. Recently, the Bolivian government has tried to stop the cultivation of coca by encouraging farmers to grow other crops. As many of the farmers have refused to convert to less profitable crops, the government has been using force to end coca cultivation.

People and Lifestyle

A Rich and Diverse Heritage

Bolivia has a population of more than 8.5 million people. The country's cultural heritage consists of a rich mix of ethnic groups and social classes. The Spanish culture brought by conquistadores in the sixteenth century has evolved alongside the ancient culture of the indigenous Amerindian groups, such as the Aymara, Quechua, and Guaraní. This mixing of cultures has produced another unique cultural heritage — that of the mestizos, people of both Amerindian and European ancestry. Bolivia's cultural landscape has also been enriched by immigrants from Germany, the Balkan region, Japan, and England, as well as Mennonites from Mexico and Paraguay. Although small in number, these communities contribute significantly to Bolivian society.

Exact figures on the ethnic composition of Bolivia are difficult to determine because of centuries of intermingling between cultures. Estimates suggest that about 55 percent of Bolivians are of Amerindian heritage, 30 percent of mestizo background, and 15 percent of European ancestry.

THE AYMARA

The second-largest Amerindian group in Bolivia, the Aymara are the descendants of the ancient Tiwanaku civilization. In spite of years of living under Incan and Spanish rule, the Aymara have kept their language and culture alive.
(*A Closer Look, page 46*)

Below: Bolivian families enjoy a meal at a shopping mall in La Paz in celebration of Mother's Day.

Adding to Bolivia's diverse ethnic culture are different social classes. The tiny upper class includes high-ranking government officials and the most successful businesspeople, most of whom have some Spanish ancestry. Members of the upper class are very wealthy and often consider themselves to be sophisticated and cultured in the European tradition. The middle class is made up of shopkeepers, doctors, teachers, engineers, and other educated professionals. A few Amerindians and many mestizos are members of the middle class. They often retain ties to their Amerindian heritage, even as they strive to fit in with the upper class. At the bottom of the social structure is a large working class — the Amerindians who work in fields, mines, and factories.

Urban and Rural Society

Bolivian society is becoming increasingly urbanized as people move from the countryside to towns and cities. In the early 1900s, less than 10 percent of the population lived in towns and cities. By the early 2000s, however, nearly 66 percent of Bolivians were living in urban areas. Bolivia's most populous cities include Santa Cruz; La Paz, which is the administrative capital of the country; El Alto; Oruro; and Cochabamba.

THE QUECHUA

The Quechua are the largest Amerindian group in Bolivia today. Quechua-speaking communities are found throughout the South American Andes.

(A Closer Look, page 66)

Family Life and Women

The family is the most important social unit in Bolivia and includes not merely parents and children but also uncles, aunts, cousins, and grandparents. This network supports members of the family in many ways, including both emotionally and financially. Bolivian women are considered the centers of their families. In addition to being wives and mothers, many are also breadwinners in certain homes. Outside the home, Bolivian women have been taking on more and more important roles. Many women in urban areas work as professionals in various fields. Women also hold important political positions in the country. Amerindian women and those living in rural areas traditionally have been active in small enterprises, such as selling food, handicrafts, and textiles. The profile of Amerindian women was raised in 1998, when Remedios Loza was elected to the Bolivian congress: she is the first woman who wears traditional Aymara dress to become a congresswoman.

Health and Living Conditions

Health care and living conditions in Bolivia are generally poor. Although medical care in the cities is adequate, the situation in the country's rural areas is far from satisfactory. Few doctors and

BERNARDO GUARACHÍ

A native of La Paz, Bernardo Guarachi became the first Bolivian, and first Amerindian, to scale to the top of Mount Everest, reaching the mountain's peak in 1998.
(A Closer Look, page 52)

Left: Newlyweds greet guests in front of a La Paz church after their wedding ceremony. The guests throw white confetti at the couple and other members of the wedding party.

nurses can be found working in rural areas. Medical services in Oriente, for example, are limited to traveling health care workers, who are not stationed permanently in the region. This area, however, is rife with diseases, such as malaria and the Chagas disease, a fatal illness spread by the vinchuca bug. The average life expectancy in Bolivia in 2003 was nearly 65 years, while the infant mortality rate was 5.6 percent. Many international aid agencies are working hard in Bolivia to improve health care.

Colorful Traditional Dress

Bolivians are known for their colorful traditional clothing, especially the traditional attire worn by Aymara women. Aymara women wear multilayered skirts called *polleras* (poh-YAY-ras), brightly colored shawls, and different styles of hats, depending on the region in which the person lives. The shawls are sometimes also used as bags to carry anything from babies to fresh market produce.

Above: **A group of Bolivian men and women sit on makeshift stands, waiting for a civic parade to begin.**

THE KALLAWAYA

For centuries, Bolivia's Amerindians have been seeing traditional healers, who use natural remedies to cure illnesses.

(A Closer Look, page 56)

Primary and Secondary Education

Primary education in Bolivia is compulsory and lasts for eight years. Students usually enter primary school when they are six or seven years old and complete their primary education by the age of fourteen.

Secondary education lasts four years and is not compulsory. Students choose either a technical or general academic program. Both programs are divided into two sections of two years each. During the first two years, courses cover subjects at a basic level, while the next two years are more specialized and go into subjects in greater depth. Students in the technical program graduate with a *Diploma de Bachiller Técnico*, while those in the general academic program graduate with a *Diploma de Bachiller Humanístico*. Secondary school graduates then have the option of attending universities.

Education for All

Bolivia faces significant challenges in educating its population. Many educational reforms have been carried out since 1955, when

Below: **Bolivian students do their homework in a park in Sucre.**

the first laws governing education were passed in the country. Today, a further series of reforms has been put in place under an initiative entitled "Education For All." Assisted by numerous local and international groups, including the World Bank and the United Nations Educational, Scientific, and Cultural Organization (UNESCO), the Bolivian government is implementing reforms that will ensure that 95 percent of Bolivian children complete primary school. Currently, less than a third of Bolivian children complete their primary education. Many of these children live in impoverished rural areas, where children need to work to help support their families. Funds allocated to the "Education For All" program in Bolivia will go toward training teachers, improving school curricula, building new schools, and providing financial assistance to children, especially those living in poor rural areas.

Above: **High school girls in Sucre walk to the bus stop after school. Most schoolgirls in Bolivia wear white uniforms.**

Higher Education

Bolivian students can pursue undergraduate and postgraduate studies at a number of higher education institutions, including public and private universities, technical colleges, and teacher training colleges. Bolivia has twelve public universities and dozens more private universities.

Religion

The official religion of Bolivia is Roman Catholicism, and some 95 percent of Bolivians belong to the Roman Catholic church. The number of Bolivian Catholics who regularly attend church services, however, is significantly less, and the number of Roman Catholic believers is also declining gradually. The remaining 5 percent of Bolivian follows a variety of faiths, including Protestant Christianity, indigenous Indian religions, Judaism, Mormonism, and the Baha'i faith. The constitution of Bolivia guarantees freedom of religion.

The Roman Catholic church in Bolivia is divided into four archdioceses, seven dioceses, two prelatures, and five vicariates. Senior church officials govern each of these divisions, which follow some of the geographic boundaries of Bolivia's various departamentos. The Bolivian Catholic church also has established various committees to address important areas, including youth, education, the family, relations with other faiths, culture, media, communication, and social justice. The Bolivian Bishop's Conference has overall responsibility for the Catholic church in the country.

Below: **Street vendors selling flowers and religious images line the outer gate of Copacabana Church near Lake Titicaca.**

Indigenous Beliefs

Roman Catholicism in Bolivia, especially as practiced by the diverse Native communities, has been influenced by indigenous Indian beliefs. The Amerindian population of the Altiplano, for example, worship Pachamama, the Goddess of the Earth, and other traditional gods. The people of Potosí and Oruro also honor Pachamama during carnival celebrations. Bolivian indigenous beliefs also have been influenced by Catholicism. For Quechua Indians, for example, the Christian cross also represents fertility and certain mountain deities.

The gods of native Bolivian religions are believed to be both human and divine, and religion is thought to help an individual develop in relationship with divine forces, as well as with other people. Indigenous beliefs teach that natural phenomena, such as rain, earthquakes, and diseases, are caused by the spirits that are associated with each of these events. Followers of indigenous religions, therefore, offer sacrifices to these supernatural forces in an attempt to control events around them. They also consult shamans for help with illnesses and other problems.

Above: Catholic devotees pray in the Church of San Francisco in La Paz.

Below: A Mennonite couple, dressed in conservative attire, pose in front of their home on the outskirts of Santa Cruz.

Language and Literature

More than thirty languages and dialects are spoken in Bolivia, but the country has just three official languages: Spanish, Aymara, and Quechua. About two-thirds of the population can speak Spanish, which is the country's main official language. Some Bolivians, mostly those of Amerindian heritage, can speak Aymara and Quechua, as well as Spanish. Bolivians living in remote communities in the highlands or lowlands of the country may not speak Spanish at all.

Indian Languages

Aymara and Quechua are the most widely used Indian languages in Bolivia. Aymara and Quechua are both spoken mainly in the western part of the country, on the Altiplano and in the Andes Mountains. Other Indian languages spoken in Bolivia include Guaraní and Chiquitano, spoken in the eastern part of the country; and Ignaciano, Cavineña, and Tacana, which are spoken in Beni.

Below: **Many Bolivians of all ages, like these three in Cochabamba, take time every day to read the newspaper.**

Left: An Aymara woman working in an office in Santa Cruz. Most present-day Aymara and Quechua people speak both their native language and Spanish.

English words derived from the Quechua vocabulary include condor, coca, llama, puma, and vicuña. The English word *jerky* comes from the Quechua word for preserved dried meat, which is *charqui* (CHAHR-kee).

Famous Writers and Literature

Bolivia has a proud literary heritage. *Ollantay*, a play that dramatizes the romance between an Inca princess and Ollanta, a general, is the most celebrated work of Quechua literature. *Pisagua*, published in 1903 by Alcides Arguedas (1879–1946), is one of the earliest Bolivian novels. Some of Arguedas's other works include *Pueblo enfermo* (1909) and *Raza de bonce* (1919), which narrate the suffering of Bolivian Indians under European rule. Another well-known Bolivian novel is *Los deshabitados*, written by Marcelo Quiroga Santa Cruz (1931–1980) and inspired by the 1952 Bolivian revolution. *Let Me Speak*, a memoir by Domitila Barrios de Chúngara, a miner's wife, describes the cruel working conditions in the Bolivian mines during the 1970s.

Arts

Pre-Columbian Arts

Bolivia's rich and diverse cultural and artistic heritage dates back more than one thousand years. The Tiwanaku civilization, centered on the Altiplano, is famous for its beautiful pottery and impressive religious buildings and sculptures. Tiwanaku temple architecture includes basalt and sandstone platforms and pyramids, decorated with carved reliefs of humanlike and animal figures, stone stelae, and tall pillars. Tiwanaku pottery is equally impressive and consists of beakers, bottles, bowls, and other vessels. Painted in black, yellow, or red, these pieces are decorated with condors, pumas, jaguars, hawks, and human heads, as well as with geometric shapes, such as triangles. Many of the faces depicted on Tiwanaku pottery have eyes that have been painted half black and half white.

The Incas, who later conquered the Tiwanaku region, carried on the tradition of monumental architecture, building impressive structures such as the Palacio del Inca on Isla del Sol, an island located in Lake Titicaca.

Above: **This detail from the painting *La Virgen del Cerro*, or *Virgin of the Hill*, contains a mixture of Indian and Spanish elements. Created in the 1700s by an anonymous artist, the portrait represents the crowning of the Virgin Mary by the Holy Trinity. Sixteenth-century European figures are painted at her feet, while smaller Inca characters appear at the base of the hill.**

Left: **An Indian girl from Tarabuco wears a handcrafted hat. The shape and design of the hat reflect both Spanish and Indian styles.**

Left: This detail is from an exquisite mestizo-baroque carving in the Church of San Lorenzo in Potosí. The church was built in the mid-1500s, at the height of the town's wealth.

Painting

The Spanish brought European culture and art to Bolivia. The fusion of Indian art and Spanish culture can be seen in Bolivia's religious art of the sixteenth century onward. Local Indian artists created paintings and sculptures and built churches in the Spanish style, using European techniques. The artists, however, added Indian touches to their religious paintings, sculptures, and architecture, creating a unique artistic style known as mestizo baroque. *Our Lady of Copacabana* is a famous example of Bolivia's mestizo baroque style. A beautiful sculpture of the Virgin Mary with the Christ Child, the work was created by Francisco Tito Yupanqui (c. 1545–1608), an Inca artist. Religious art using gold and silver, abundant minerals in Bolivia, continued to develop during the colonial period. *La Ultima Cena* (The Last Supper), a remarkable silver relief, was created in the early 1700s.

Contemporary Bolivian painters include Maria Louisa Pacheco (1918–1982), Gil Imaná (1933–), Oscar Pantoja (1925–), and Alfredo La Placa (1939–).

MARINA NÚÑEZ DEL PRADO

A world-renowned sculptor, Marina Núñez del Prado is one of Bolivia's most famous artists.
(A Closer Look, page 62)

Music and Dance

Music and dance are important parts of Bolivian culture, and both art forms have a long history in the country. The indigenous peoples of the Altiplano and the Andes had a rich tradition of music long before the Incan conquest of the region. Traditional instruments that have been played for centuries in the country include flutes, trumpets, and drums, many of which have been found in ancient tombs and at other archaeological sites.

New musical instruments were introduced to Bolivia by the Spanish. These include the *charango* (cha-RAHN-goh), which is a small guitar made from the shell of an armadillo, and the harp, violin, and mandolin. Traditional Bolivian flutes include the *quena* (KEH-nah) and the *siku* (SEE-koo), which resembles panpipes. These flutes are used to perform contemporary Bolivian folk music, which, along with folk music from other countries of the Andes, has become very popular in Europe, Japan, and the United States. Several Bolivian musical groups have become world famous, including Savia Andina and Rumillajta.

Below: **Aymara men play the *tarka* (TAHR-kah), a traditional wind instrument, during a festival in La Paz.**

Dancing is a major part of Bolivian festivals and celebrations. Traditional Aymara dances include the *sikuri* (see-KOOH-ree), which is also the name for music performed by a group of siku players, and the *cueca* (KWAY-kah) and *huayño* (WHY-nyo). The cueca and the huayño are performed by couples.

Above: **Bolivians wearing colorful outfits dance during the Festival of Santa Rosa in Potosí.**

Museums and Cultural Institutes

Bolivia's rich artistic scene is supported by many museums and cultural institutes. Major museums in La Paz include the National Museum of Art, the National Museum of Archaeology, and the Casa de Murillo ethnographic museum. La Paz also houses the Kusillo Children's Museum. Numerous private art galleries, theaters, and museums dot Bolivia's major cities. These venues host exhibitions of textiles, metalwork, contemporary painting, sculpture, and jewelry, as well as highlight Bolivia's traditional artistic heritage. Exhibitions and arts performances are also held at other cultural institutes in La Paz, including the Bolivian American Center, British Council, Goethe Institute, and L'Alliance Française, which is a French cultural center.

33

Leisure and Festivals

How Bolivians spend their leisure time depends to some extent on income, social class, and place of residence. In general, however, Bolivians, like people in other parts of the world, like to spend their leisure time socializing with friends and family, while engaging in a variety of activities.

Evenings in the highlands are chilly, so clubs and bars there tend to close earlier than their counterparts in the tropical lowlands, where warm temperatures encourage residents to stay out longer. Bolivians living in cities and towns, especially those from the wealthier classes, have a wide range of leisure and recreational options to choose from, including going to Internet cafés and discotheques, eating at different types of restaurants, and watching satellite television. These options are usually not available in rural areas, although televisions and telephone service are increasingly common in rural Bolivia. Rich Bolivians

Below: **Boys play the popular game of foosball, called** *futbolín* **(foot-boh-LEAN) in Bolivia, in Betanzos.**

may shop at supermarkets in the wealthier suburbs of Bolivia's cities, while poorer Bolivians frequent the cheaper open markets. Regardless of where they shop, Bolivians consider shopping a form of recreation during which they meet with friends and catch up with the latest gossip. Going to a movie is another popular pastime in Bolivia's towns and cities.

Above: **A father watches his daughters play at a park in La Paz.**

Games

Sapo (SAH-poh), which is the Spanish word for "toad," is a popular game played at outdoor restaurants in Bolivia. Participants try to shoot tokens into the mouth of a small metal toad. Bolivian women like to play card games such as canasta or rummy. Some married men go out together to play *cacho* (KAH-choh), a dice game, or various card games, and have a drink at the local bar every Friday. This weekly outing is commonly referred to as *viernes de soltero* (bee-EHR-nehs deh sol-TEH-roh), or "bachelor's Friday." Children's toys include tops called *trompos* (TROHM-pohs), marbles, dolls, and slingshots. Foosball is also a popular game among boys.

Sports

Soccer is the most popular sport in Bolivia. The sport is governed at the national level by the Federacíon Boliviana de Fútbol, or Bolivian Football Association. Based in the city of Cochabamba, the association was founded in 1925 and became a member of the Fédération Internationale de Football Association (FIFA) in 1926. FIFA is the world body that governs the sport of soccer. Well-known soccer teams in Bolivia include Oriente Petrolero, Real Santa Cruz, Blooming, The Strongest, Bolívar, Jorge Wilstermann, and San Luis de Potosí.

Bolivian soccer teams participate in regional competitions, such as the Copa Mercosur, Copa Toyota Libertadores, and Copa Sudamericana. Bolivia's national soccer team also takes part in many regional and international competitions, including the Copa América; the Campeonata Sudamericano Sub-17, for teams of players under the age of seventeen; and the World Cup competitions. Bolivia's women's soccer team takes part in the Sudamericano Feminina competition for South American women's soccer teams.

The Bolivian national soccer team's performance in international and regional soccer has been mixed. Successes

Below: **Amerindian women, some in full skirts, play a game of soccer in Copacabana.**

Left: **Bolivian Fabio Gutierrez (*right*) guides the ball past three Colombian players in a World Cup qualifying match in April 2000 in La Paz. The two teams tied the match 1–1.**

include qualifying for the World Cup competition in 1994 and reaching the finals of the Copa América in 1997. Famous Bolivian soccer stars include Marco Etcheverry, who plays for the U.S. soccer team D.C. United, Ramiro Castillo, and Demetrio Angola.

Countless Bolivians play soccer in stadiums and fields throughout the country. The Tahuichi Academy, founded by Rolando Aguilera Pareja in 1978, is a famous soccer academy in Bolivia. The academy has trained more than one thousand players since its founding, including Marco Etcheverry. Tahuichi Academy accepts children from poor families who show the potential to become talented soccer players and provides them with soccer training and an education.

Other Sports

Other sporting activities that are popular in Bolivia include cycling, boxing, volleyball, basketball, and automobile racing. In the 2003 Pan American Games, Bolivian cyclist Benjamin Martinez won a bronze medal, while women racquetball players Paola Nuñez and Carola Loma Santos won a bronze medal in the doubles event of their sport. Bolivian athletes Rosa Apaza, Geovana Irusta, and Ariana Quino also competed in events at the 2003 Pan American Games.

Holidays and Festivals

Bolivian festivals are colorful affairs that feature much music and dancing. Many religious holidays are also occasions for great celebration. One of the most festive times in the Bolivian calendar falls between February and March, when pre-Lenten carnivals take place throughout the country. The carnival celebrations of Oruro are some of Bolivia's most spectacular cultural events. Thousands of dancers and musicians in colorful costumes take to the streets of the city, culminating in a grand, daylong procession called *entrada* (en-TRAH-dah). Some costumes feature elaborate masks made from a variety of materials, including cloth, plaster, tin cans, and brightly colored feathers. Lively dances performed during the carnival include the *morenada* (more-ren-NAH-dah) and the *diablada* (dee-ah-BLAH-dah). Dancers of the diablada wear frightening masks that depict devils. The morenada portrays the suffering of African slaves who were brought to Bolivia to work in the colonial Spanish mines. Dancers representing Spanish colonists are shown leading other dancers who represent African slaves.

Below: Devotees gather around the statue of the Virgin of Copacabana during the festival that takes place each August on the shores of Lake Titicaca. This festival honors the Virgin Mary.

Above: A man dressed as a devil takes part in a parade held in the city of Copacabana.

Festivals celebrated in Cochabamba include the feast of the Virgin of Copacabana and the feast of the Virgin of Urkupiña. Both festivals take place in August and include vibrant folk dances, lively music, and colorful processions.

Semana Santa (seh-MAH-nah SAHN-tah), or Holy Week, is an important religious festival that takes place throughout Bolivia in March or April. The festivities include a pilgrimage from La Paz to Copacabana, in which hundreds of Bolivians journey to the city on foot and arrive on Good Friday.

La Paz celebrates the festival of El Gran Poder in late May or early June. A holiday dedicated to Jesus Christ, El Gran Poder features colorful processions and competitions for the best music and dance groups. Other religious festivals include feast days devoted to various patron saints of towns and cities, including the feasts of San Lorenzo, San Joaquin, San Ignacio, and San Francisco. Christmas is celebrated on December 25.

Todos Santos (TOE-dose SAHN-tose), or All Saints' Day, is a religious holiday that honors the souls of the dead. During the first two days in November, Bolivians all over the country visit the graves of their loved ones and decorate the tombstones with colorful garlands of flowers.

SECULAR HOLIDAYS

Secular holidays in Bolivia include New Year's Day on January 1, Independence Day on August 6, and Labor Day on May 1. On the second Sunday of March, the town of Tarabuco, in Sucre, celebrates a festival to commemorate the victory of local tribes over Spanish troops in 1816.

Food

Bolivian cuisine makes use of the country's incredible range of agricultural produce, which includes the more than one hundred varieties of potatoes grown in the region; quinoa, a highly nutritious grain cultivated in the highlands; several kinds of peppers; and *quirquiña* (keer-KEEN-nya), a type of indigenous herb. Bolivia's culinary heritage is further enriched by the mixture of Spanish and Indian styles of cooking.

Typical Bolivian meals feature meat, rice or potatoes, and vegetables. Wealthier families and those living in the cities might have several courses, consisting of soups and salads, followed by a main dish and dessert. Peppers, called *ají* (ah-HEE), used either in dried form or mixed to make sauces, add spice to various Bolivian dishes. Varieties of ají include the *locoto* (loh-KOH-toe), *ulupica* (ooh-loo-PEE-kah), and *aji amarillo* (ah-HEE ah-mah-REE-yoh).

Below: **Bolivians buy freshly baked bread from street bakers in Tarija. Bolivian bread is made from several varieties of wheat.**

Soups

Typical Bolivian soups are rich, nutritious, and satisfying. *Chupe de papaliza* (CHOO-pay day pah-pah-LEE-zah) is a soup made from a yellow potato called papaliza, broad beans, and squash. The ingredients for *ch'aque de quinua* (chah-KAY day KEEN-wah) consist of quinoa, potatoes, tomatoes, leeks, carrots, and broad beans.

Meat Dishes

Bolivian meat dishes include chicken and pork stews, roast pig, spicy chicken dishes, rice and meat dishes, and meat turnovers called *salteñas* (sahl-TEHN-nyas). Salteñas contain meat, olives, and eggs and are flavored with spicy red peppers, cumin, oregano, parsley, and ground black pepper. These ingredients are wrapped in a pastry made from flour, margarine, and eggs.

Other meat dishes include *saici* (SYE-see), which is a spicy meat dish, and *majao* (ma-JOW), a dish of rice and meat served with fried plantain, egg, and cassava. The meat used in majao can either be roast beef or beef jerky.

A CLOSER LOOK AT BOLIVIA

Bolivia is a country blessed with spectacular natural landscapes, rich and ancient cultures, and warm and friendly people. For many years, Bolivia was considered a remote destination. This impression may have helped the country preserve its natural beauty and artistic traditions.

In recent years, numerous tourists have discovered Bolivia's unique natural and historical attractions. The imposing Andes Mountains attract mountain climbers from many countries, and trekkers and adventurers seek the challenge of scaling Illimani and Huayna Potosí, two well-known Bolivian peaks.

Opposite: **A masked woman celebrates the Festival of the Virgin in Copacabana, near Lake Titicaca.**

The country's mountains are also home to the highest capital in the world, La Paz, as well as the highest navigable lake in the world, Lake Titicaca. Other fascinating sites in Bolivia include the ruins of the Tiwanaku empire near the shores of Titicaca and dinosaur footprints at Cal Orko. Some visitors come in search of the legendary lost city of Atlantis, or to experience the cures of Bolivia's natural healers, the Kallawaya. Bolivia is also the home of notable figures such as Bernardo Guarachi, the first Amerindian to reach the top of Mount Everest, and Marina Núñez del Prado, an outstanding contemporary sculptor.

Above: **Bolivians love music and dance. Even young children are able to play traditional musical instruments, such as the panpipes.**

Atlantis in Bolivia

The myth of Atlantis, an ancient civilization swallowed up by the sea, has intrigued people for more than two thousand years. The Greek philosopher Plato first described Atlantis in two of his dialogues, *Timaeus* and *Critias*. According to Plato, Atlantis had existed more than nine thousand years earlier, until a series of earthquakes and floods sunk the city into the sea. Plato described Atlantis as a prosperous empire located opposite the Strait of Gibraltar, the narrow passage between southern Spain and northern Africa that he termed the Pillars of Hercules. Plato said the empire was located on an island larger than Africa and Asia combined.

The main city of Atlantis was described as being surrounded by a flat oblong plain, which was in turn surrounded by striking mountains. Located 5 miles (8 km) from the sea, the land was rich in fruit-bearing trees and was home to wealthy villages. The people of Atlantis had built a canal from the sea to the center of the island. A temple dedicated to the Greek god of the sea, Poseidon, was built on the island. The walls of this temple were allegedly covered with silver, gold, and the alloy orichalcum.

Below: **Sand dunes on the Altiplano may hide the remains of the mythical city of Atlantis.**

The Altiplano: The Location of Atlantis?

According to British cartographer Jim Allen, author of *Atlantis: The Andes Solution*, Plato's description of Atlantis fits many of the characteristics of the Bolivian Altiplano. Using satellite photography, Allen determined that the Altiplano is indeed oblong in shape and located 5 miles (8 km) from a body of water, Lake Poopó. An Amerindian legend describes a city that sunk into the rising waters of a lake, a story similar to Plato's description of the sinking of Atlantis.

Most scholars today question Allen's theories, even though there are many similarities between Plato's Atlantis and the Bolivian Altiplano. Some believe that the myth of Atlantis stems from the Minoan civilization on the Mediterranean island of Crete. This civilization was destroyed by a volcanic explosion on the nearby island of Santorini in the fifteenth century B.C. The Bolivian Altiplano, however, will continue to attract scholars in search of the lost continent of Atlantis.

The Aymara

Descendants of the Tiwanaku Civilization

The Aymara are an Amerindian people with a heritage that dates back to the great Tiwanaku civilization. Today, Aymara populations can be found in parts of Argentina, Bolivia, and Peru. In Bolivia, the Aymara form about 25 percent of the country's population and are concentrated in the region near Lake Titicaca.

Into the Twenty-First Century

Bolivia's Aymara are divided between the country's urban and rural areas. Many rural Aymara are subsistence farmers and lead their lives according to traditional agricultural cycles and activities. Most of them do not own tractors or oxen and continue to work on their plots using traditional tools, such as the foot plow, as their early ancestors did. Aymara farmers also faithfully follow a pattern of crop rotation that has been tried and tested for generations. Potatoes are the most important crop to the Aymara, who also grow corn, quinoa, and barley. Because the Aymara consider the act of planting sacred, only women, who are regarded as the givers of life, are allowed to perform the task. Aymara herders typically look after flocks of llamas, alpacas, and sheep, which provide both wool and meat.

Left: A young Aymara couple take in a bird's-eye view of La Paz from a nearby mountain.

Urban Aymara sharply contrast with their rural counterparts. Their lifestyles are more modern and often more Western. Many urban Aymara attend universities and work as doctors, lawyers, engineers, or members of other professions.

Above: **The bowler hats Aymara women wear easily distinguish them from other Amerindian women.**

Aymara Life and Culture

The Aymara in Bolivia's cities may live in modern buildings and apartments, but many rural Aymara still live in adobe huts with thatch roofs. Adobe is sun-dried brick made from a mixture of clay and straw. A typical Aymara home in the country consists of one multipurpose room that is about 80 square feet (7 square m) in size. One end of the house is designated as the sleeping area, while the other end serves as the cooking area. The Aymara still use clay stoves for cooking. Spicy stews or soups are typical Aymara meals.

Maintaining strong family ties is an important aspect of Aymara life. The basic family unit in Aymara society is extended and consists of parents, unmarried children, and grandparents living in one house. Large rural families often divide into several houses built near one another. In urban areas, members of Aymara families may choose to live close to one another as well.

QUINOA

Quinoa is a grain indigenous to the South American Andes, and the Aymara have been eating quinoa for centuries. In Aymara food, quinoa usually is used in thick soups or ground into flour to make bread. Quinoa is high in protein and extremely nutritious. Today, quinoa can be found in health food shops around the world.

Simón Bolívar

The Man Who Inspired Bolivia

Simón Bolívar is widely regarded as *El Libertador* (EHL lee-behr-tah-DOHR), or "the Liberator," in countries such as Bolivia, Colombia, Ecuador, Panama, Peru, and Venezuela. Born on July 24, 1783, Bolívar spent much of his adult life trying to free parts of Central and South America from the clutches of the Spanish crown. A well-educated nobleman with no formal military training, Bolívar suffered numerous setbacks in his resistance efforts against the Spanish, but his remarkable determination eventually led to success.

In 1825, Bolívar's forces entered the territory of present-day Bolivia, which was known as Upper Peru at that time, and lent support to the region's ongoing struggle for autonomy. That same year, Upper Peru was declared an independent state and renamed in honor of Bolívar.

Left: **Statues and monuments of El Libertador abound in city and town squares throughout South America. Simón Bolívar is also known as the "George Washington of South America" to some people.**

Left: Simón Bolívar was born in Caracas, Venezuela, to a wealthy family of Spanish aristocratic descent. Bolívar's parents died when he was nine years old, and he came under the care of an uncle, who later sent him to Spain to pursue his education. While in Europe, Bolívar dreamed of a unified and independent Latin America. During a trip to Italy, while standing on top of Mount Aventin in Rome, Bolívar made a vow to never rest until South America was free from Spanish domination. On December 17, 1830, after years of battling political disunity within the area known as Gran Colombia and rebellions in the newly formed South American states, Simón Bolívar died poor and disillusioned in Colombia. Gran Colombia was a union of present-day Colombia, Ecuador, Panama, and Venezuela Bolívar formed in 1819.

Bolivia and South American Independence

In the early 1800s, Spain suffered a mighty blow when French forces led by Napoleon invaded the country. Spanish colonies in Latin America then took advantage of the Spanish crown's weakness and revolted against the local Spanish authorities.

In South America, quests for autonomy began at both ends of the continent. Simón Bolívar led the resistance movement in the north, while José de San Martín, an Argentine national hero, did the same in the south. By 1822, when Bolívar met with San Martín in Ecuador, Peru was the main seat of Spanish power in South America, sandwiched between Bolívar's and San Martín's armies. After the meeting, Bolívar and his forces began to play a more active role in the liberation of Peru and Upper Peru than San Martín and his men.

In 1824, Antonio José de Sucre, one of Bolívar's lieutenants, won the Battle of Ayacucho in Peru. The victory swept aside the last traces of Spanish power in South America, and in 1825, Sucre defeated the remaining Spanish forces in Upper Peru. In August 1825, Upper Peru became the independent republic of Bolivia. Bolívar wrote the country's first constitution, and Sucre became Bolivia's first president.

Dinosaur Footprints

Dinosaurs lived on Earth in the Mesozoic era, which occurred from approximately 245 million to 65 million years ago. Scientists have learned much about dinosaurs from the large number of fossilized dinosaur bones found in many parts of the world. Additional information about dinosaurs comes from the footprints, or tracks, these animals left behind. These footprints, which are also fossilized, show how and where dinosaurs roamed, what their postures and gaits were like, and whether or not they traveled in herds.

Bolivia's Dinosaur Footprints

Bolivia is home to the largest collection of dinosaur footprints in the world. Discovered in the 1990s by a group of Bolivian scientists working at Cal Orcko Canyon, near Sucre, the site has so far revealed about 250 sets of footprints extending over an area of some 269,098 square feet (25,000 sq m). Scientists believe the dinosaur footprints were made nearly seventy million years ago.

Below: **Like the site in Cal Orcko, the land on which these dinosaur tracks are found has been tilted up by geological movements to form a steep hill.**

The footprints found at Cal Orcko are embedded along the side of a hill. However, scientists believe that the area was previously a lake, where dinosaurs came for food and water. The bed of the lake was eventually pushed up by geological movements, producing a steep hill. The dinosaurs were probably walking on the muddy shores of the lake when they left the footprints, which eventually hardened into fossils.

Above: **Dinosaur footprints can be found throughout Bolivia. These tracks are located in a valley near Cochabamba.**

Walking With Dinosaurs

The dinosaur footprints, some as long as 3 feet (91 cm), range from those of the titanosaur, an herbivore that could be as tall as 82 feet (25 m), to those of smaller carnivorous dinosaurs. Titanosaurs were quadrupedal, meaning they walked on four legs, while the smaller carnivorous dinosaurs were bipedal, walking on two legs. By studying their footprints, scientists can determine, for example, whether a dinosaur was limping or traveling at a high speed of more than 19 miles (30 km) per hour. One set of dinosaur tracks at the Cal Orcko site continues for 383 yards (350 m), which, at present, makes it the longest recorded set of dinosaur tracks in the world.

Bernardo Guarachi

Bernardo Guarachi is one of Bolivia's most famous mountain climbers and mountain guides. An Aymara Indian, Guarachi was born on December 4, 1952, in Patacamaya, an Altiplano village southwest of La Paz. In 1972, Guarachi became a porter to foreign trekkers and mountain climbers. Impressed by the young porter's dedication to his job, the German Alpine Club arranged for Guarachi to travel to the Alps to receive professional training as a mountain guide and instructor.

In 1974, Guarachi climbed his first Bolivian peak. Since then, Guarachi has accumulated an impressive record of achievements. He has climbed to the top of the 21,201-foot (6,462-m) Mount Illimani in La Paz more than 170 times. He has also climbed Mount Aconcagua, the highest peak in the Americas at 22,831 feet (6,959 m), three times. Guarachi has also taken groups of trekkers to the tops of some of his home country's highest peaks, including Sajama and Huayna Potosí, over one hundred times.

Left: **Former president Hugo Bánzer Suárez (*far right*) hands a Bolivian flag to Bernardo Guarachi (*far left*) on March 5, 1997, during a reception to celebrate Guarachi's plans to climb Mount Everest the following year. On May 25, 1998, the Bolivian flag flew high from the summit of Mount Everest.**

Because of his stamina and expertise, Guarachi was hired by Eastern Airlines for a rescue mission in 1985. He was the first mountain climber to arrive at the scene of the fatal crash of an Eastern Airlines jet on Mount Illimani that year. Guarachi also rescued an injured man much heavier than himself off Huayna Potosí. In 1992, he was involved in the search and recovery of the bodies of six Chilean mountain climbers who had died trying to climb Mount Illimani on their own.

In 1994, Guarachi climbed the Himalayan mountain Makalu (27,766 feet/8,463 m). That same year, he attempted to reach the summit of Mount Everest. However, strong winds and blizzards forced him and his team to abort the expedition. Four years later, Guarachi returned to Mount Everest. In the early morning hours of May 25, 1998, Bernardo Guarachi became the first Bolivian and the first Amerindian to set foot on top of Mount Everest, the highest mountain in the world at 29,035 feet (8,850 m). Upon returning to Bolivia, Bernardo Guarachi received the Cóndor de los Andes award, his country's highest distinction. A postage stamp bearing his face was also issued in his honor.

Above: **Bernardo Guarachi poses for the camera after reaching the top of Mount Condoriri (18,530 feet/5,648 m) in the Cordillera Real in 2000.**

Illimani and Huayna Potosí

Nicknamed the "Two Andean Queens," Illimani and Huayna Potosí are the two highest peaks of the Cordillera Real. The Cordillera Real forms part of the Bolivian Andes. Local and international mountain-climbing enthusiasts organize frequent expeditions to scale the two well-loved Bolivian peaks. The period from May to September is generally accepted as the best time for mountain climbing in Bolivia because of the stable and dry winter climate (winter in Bolivia lasts from June to August). Rainfall in the mountains, which turns any expedition into a dangerous activity, is more frequent in the hotter months.

Illimani

Permanently snowcapped, Illimani is the highest peak in the Cordillera Real, but few sources agree on its height. Estimates range from 20,741 feet (6,322 m) to 21,201 feet (6,462 m). The reason for this disagreement could be that Illimani is a massif,

Below: Paceños (pah-SEH-neos), the residents of La Paz, are always reminded of the towering presence of Illimani.

Left: Huayna Potosí, as seen from Mount Condoriri, towers over other peaks in the Cordillera Real.

a compressed section of a mountain range that contains several summits, rather than a single mountain. Geologically, Illimani is composed of seven peaks, all of which are over 19,686 feet (6,000 m) in height. Because of its towering presence over La Paz, Illimani was given the nickname "Guardian of the City." The name "Illimani," however, means the "Shining One."

Huayna Potosí

Most sources agree that Huayna Potosí rises to a height of about 19,975 feet (6,088 m). Snowcapped for much of the year, Huayna Potosí is the closest of the Cordillera Real mountains to the city of La Paz. Many experienced climbers believe that climbing Huayna Potosí is a good training exercise for people who wish to climb Illimani. One mountaineering school arranges for its students to be driven from La Paz to a base camp near Huayna Potosí. From there, the students and their guides hike for two to three hours to reach the edge of a glacier that rests at an altitude of about 16,897 feet (5,150 m). Crossing the glacier takes about two hours and takes students up to a height of 18,045 feet (5,500 m), where a second camp is located. After some food and ample rest, the students and their guides spend the next eight to ten hours making their way to the top of Huayna Potosí.

ILLIMANI IN HISTORY

In 1877, Charles Weiner, a French scientist, made history by seeking to estimate Illimani's height. Weiner had scaled one of Illimani's southern peaks with several Bolivian Amerindians, who later helped him record the atmospheric pressure at the summit. With the recorded figures, Weiner was able to calculate the altitude of the terrain on which they were standing — 20,729 feet (6,318 m). Weiner discovered that, up until that time, no one had reached such heights before. In 1898, Englishman Baron Conway became the first person to climb to the top of Illimani.

55

The Kallawaya

Traveling Healers

For hundreds of years, the Kallawaya of Bolivia have traveled from region to region using special herbs and rituals to cure diseases. They are the country's natural healers. Traditionally always men, these healers pass their knowledge from father to son. Although the Kallawaya live on the Altiplano, they have traveled to other parts of South America, bringing their herbal remedies to all corners of the Inca empire. Today, both rural and urban Bolivians call on the Kallawaya for healing.

Kallawaya Cures

The Kallawaya use many different kinds of herbs and plants to cure their patients. Scholars believe that the Kallawaya were among the first healers to cure malaria, an illness transmitted by the bite of a tropical mosquito, using quinine, a substance extracted from the bark of the cinchona tree. Modern-day Western doctors still use quinine to treat malaria. The Kallawaya treat heartburn with a special tea made with dandelion leaves. Dried

Below: **A Kallawaya healer often carries his bundle of herbs in a colorful shawl.**

Above: **Outdoor markets throughout Bolivia sell special herbs to cure different ailments, ranging from stomach ulcers to depression.**

dandelion roots also are used to treat wounds. Before suggesting remedies, the Kallawaya talk with their patients to gather information about the environments in which the patients live and their diets. Kallawaya treatment is holistic, which means that the Kallawaya believe a person's health depends on both the proper functioning of the body and good emotional and spiritual health.

Preserving Ethnobotanical Knowledge

Today, the younger generation of Kallawaya may not be as interested as the older generation were in learning about traditional medicine. To preserve Bolivia's ethnobotanical knowledge, the country's Center for Comprehensive Training and Services for Development (CISED) tries to record the oral traditions of the Kallawaya healers. In this way, CISED documents the traditional ethnobotanical knowledge of the Kallawaya. Ethnobotany is the study of the knowledge accumulated by an ethnic group about the plants and trees growing around them and how this group views and uses plants in their daily lives.

Lake Titicaca

Located in the northern section of the Andes Mountains, Lake Titicaca is famous for being the world's highest navigable lake. Resting at 12,500 feet (3,810 m) above sea level, the lake covers an area of about 3,200 square miles (8,288 square km). Lake Titicaca is about 120 miles (193 km) long and about 50 miles (80 km) across at its widest point.

Between Bolivia and Peru

Lake Titicaca is flanked by Bolivia, which lies to its east, and Peru, which lies to its west. Located near the southeastern end of the lake and within Bolivian territory, the Strait of Tiquina, formed by the Copacabana Peninsula to the west and the Bolivian mainland to the east, divides the lake into northwestern and southeastern sections. Bolivians know the smaller southeastern section as Huiñaymarca and the larger section as Lake Chucuito, while Peruvians know them as Lake Chucuito and Lake Grande, respectively.

HOW THE LAKE GAINS AND LOSES WATER

Lake Titicaca is supported by more than twenty-five rivers that empty their waters into its pool. Desaguadero, a small river that originates at the southwestern tip of the lake, is the only river that drains the lake. Lake Titicaca loses more water, however, through evaporation caused by strong, dry winds and intense heat from the sun.

Left: A totora reed boat meant for tourists is anchored at Titicaca Island. Lake Titicaca is home to more than forty islands, the largest of which is Titicaca Island. Also known as Isla del Sol, which means "Island of the Sun," Titicaca Island is located within Bolivian territory, just off the tip of the Copacabana Peninsula. Lying to the southeast of Titicaca Island is Isla de la Luna, or "Island of the Moon." Inca ruins have been found on both islands.

The floor of Lake Titicaca forms a sharp incline, with the eastern side of the lake significantly deeper than the western side. The lake has average depths that range between 460 and 600 feet (140 and 183 m), but nearer its eastern shores, the lake has depths of up to 920 feet (280 m).

Opposite: Inca ruins still stand at Tiwanaku, a historical site in Bolivian territory, located at the southwestern tip of Lake Titicaca.

Life In, On, and Around the Lake

A few fish species, including catfish (*Trichomycterus*) and killifish (*Orestias*), thrive in the lake's brackish, or slightly salty, waters. Trout are commonly caught in the lake, but the species is not native to Lake Titicaca, having been introduced in the late 1930s.

The Uru people have a unique way of life that dates back to ancient times. They make their homes on mats of densely packed, dried totora that float on the lake's waters, as their ancestors did centuries ago. The Uru are also keepers of the special knowledge that teaches them how to make large, crescent-shaped boats by tying bundles of totora reeds together. Today, the Uru make a living from fishing and transporting goods across the lake using their totora reed boats.

Communities of Aymara-speaking people inhabit the shores of the lake. Mostly farmers, the Aymara mainly grow potatoes and barley and rear livestock, such as llamas and alpacas, for food. Llamas and alpacas are South American cousins of the camel.

MARACAIBO OR TITICACA?

Most sources identify Lake Titicaca as South America's second-largest lake, after Lake Maracaibo in Venezuela. Lake Titicaca, however, is signifcantly deeper than its Venezuelan counterpart and contains much more water. The only reason Lake Maracaibo is recognized as the continent's largest lake is because it has a larger surface area, at about 5,130 square miles (13,287 square km).

National Parks and Other Protected Areas

Bolivia is home to national parks and nature reserves that protect the country's rich ecological heritage. Protected areas within Bolivia include Amboró National Park, Madidi National Park, and Noel Kempff Mercado National Park

Amboró National Park

Located west of Santa Cruz and covering an area of more than 1.56 million acres (637,600 hectares), Amboró National Park supports several ecosystems, including the cool low mountainous areas of the Andes; tropical rain forests; and the subtropical woodlands, thorn forests, and grasslands of the northern Chaco region. A huge range of plant and animal species can be found in these diverse habitats. South America's only bear species, the rare spectacled bear, lives in Amboró National Park. To date, 638 species of trees and plants have been identified in the national park, including hardwood trees such as mahogany and various

Below: **Amboró National Park, in eastern Bolivia, is home to several hundred species of birds.**

Left: **Thatched huts serve as lookout points that allow ecotourists bird's-eye views of the surrounding areas.**

types of orchids, palms, giant fern, and bamboo. Amboró National Park also supports a large number of bird species, including the horned curassow, the chestnut-fronted macaw, and the cuvier toucan.

Noel Kempff Mercado National Park

Bolivia's Noel Kempff Mercado National Park is a World Heritage Site. The park's more than 3.76 million acres (1.5 million hectares) support a rich diversity of both habitats and plant and animal species, some of which are rare or endangered.

Located in the northeastern corner of Bolivia near the border with Brazil, the park features a range of habitats, including evergreen forests, deciduous forests, savannas, and wetlands. These rich ecosystems are home to 150 species of mammals, more than 620 bird species, and 74 reptile species, as well as numerous amphibians, fish, and insects. Scientists have also identified about 4,000 species of plants growing in the park. Noel Kempff Mercado National Park boasts many of Bolivia's large mammals, including the tapir, jaguar, pampas deer, maned wolf, brocket deer, and marsh deer.

A description of the park's beauty and diversity by Percy Fawcett in 1910 later inspired Sir Arthur Conan Doyle to base his novel *The Lost World* on this fascinating region.

Marina Núñez del Prado

Marina Núñez del Prado (1910–1995) is a world-renowned sculptor, whose works can be found in numerous museums. Her sculptures reflect her love for her homeland, Bolivia.

Her Life

Núñez del Prado was born in La Paz in 1910. She studied plastic arts at the Fine Arts Academy in La Paz and became a professor of art anatomy and sculpture at the academy a year after her graduation. She became the first woman to be appointed chair of art anatomy and sculpture during her seven-year career with the academy. In 1938, she left the academy and later lived and worked in many countries, including Italy, France, and the United States. During this long period of touring, she held exhibitions, participated in art events, and won numerous awards and honors. She returned to Bolivia in 1948 to continue her work. In 1972, she moved to Peru, where she spent the remaining years of her life with her husband, Peruvian writer Jorge Falcon.

Below: **Marina Núñez del Prado poses among her sculptures in her studio in Lima, Peru.**

Left: **Núñez del Prado's abstract sculptures often represent stylized female figures. She was particularly interested in sculpting images that show the strong and close relationship between a mother and child.**

Her Work

Núñez del Prado's work is characterized by curves and abstract forms. The smooth curves of her sculptures represent the undulating Bolivian mountains and the strong human spirit of the Aymara Indians. Two of her pieces are *White Venus* and *Mother and Child*. Both pieces are sculptured from white onyx, which is a kind of quartz. Núñez del Prado chose the materials she sculptured carefully. White onyx is said to symbolize the enduring quality of motherhood. She also sculptured from black granite, alabaster, basalt, and native Bolivian woods.

Núñez del Prado Museum

The Casa Museo Núñez del Prado in La Paz was Núñez del Prado's family home. It was donated to the Bolivian people and converted into a museum in 1984. The museum is home to the largest collection of pieces by Núñez del Prado. More than a thousand of her sculptures and drawings are on display.

Privatization of Water in Cochabamba

Rising Water Prices

In September 1999, the Bolivian government sold off the water and sanitation services of Cochabamba to Aguas del Tunari, a company owned by several multinational corporations, including U.S.-based Bechtel Corporation and U.K.-based International Water Limited. Aguas del Tunari promised to upgrade the water supply system of Cochabamba so that more people could have access to clean water and modern sewage facilities. The company also planned to provide water for irrigation. In order to make these improvements, however, Aguas del Tunari announced that it would raise the water rates. For some residents of the area, water bills doubled or tripled. Many families found that up to half of their monthly income went toward paying for water.

Below: **A Bolivian riot police officer, wearing an anti-tear gas mask, patrols Cochabamba's main square during the water protests of February 2000.**

La Coordinadora's Campaign

In February 2000, a grassroots group called La Coordinadora gathered some Cochabamba residents for a march to protest the increased water prices. La Coordinadora demanded that Aguas del Tunari leave their city and that management of the water supply system be handed over to La Coordinadora. Over the course of the next few months, the protests grew larger and larger. At first, the demonstrations, led by union organizer Oscar Olivera, were peaceful, but they soon turned violent. The Bolivian Army stepped in, and a young protester was killed in April 2000.

After months of protests, President Hugo Bánzer signed an agreement with Oscar Olivera to hand over control of Cochabamba's water supply to La Coordinadora. The Bolivian government terminated its contract with Aguas del Tunari, and the company was forced to leave Cochabamba. The agreement marked a victory for the people of Cochabamba. La Coordinadora, led by Olivera, hopes to ensure that the city's water supply stays under public control. The next challenge for the group will be to prove to the people of Cochabamba that they can not only fight for their water supply but also manage it properly.

The Quechua

Natives of the Andean Highlands

The Quechua are an Amerindian people who have inhabited parts of the Altiplano since pre-Incan times. These Natives of the highlands had already formed agriculturally based communities by the early 1400s, when the Chanca invaded the region. Since then, the Quechua have had to endure nearly five centuries of foreign domination. After the Chanca invaded, the Quechua became part of the Incan Empire. By the 1530s, they began three hundred years of servitude to the Spanish colonists.

In Bolivia today, the Quechua and Quechua-speakers make up about 30 percent of the country's population and number significantly in the regions of Chuquisaca, Cochabamba, Oruro, Potosí, and Tarija.

QUECHUA OR QUECHUA-SPEAKERS?

The Quechua speak a language known by the same name. Today, the term "Quechua" is likely to refer to a mixture of Quechua people and non-Quechua peoples who speak only the Quechua language. Some believe it is more accurate to refer to the mixed population as "Quechua-speakers."

Because Quechua was the official language of the Incan Empire, non-Quechua groups had to learn the language in order to trade and communicate within the empire. The Spanish colonists who replaced the Incas continued to use Quechua as a common language between themselves and the different Andean peoples they controlled. The languages of some of these peoples became extinct after centuries of disuse, and much of their cultural identities and roots were also lost. Without their own language and unable to account for their backgrounds, they became identified as Quechua over time.

Left: A legacy of the Incan Empire, these steps on Isla del Sol, or Island of the Sun, are part of a sacred site many Bolivian Quechua believe is where founders of the Incan Empire were created by the sun god. Small Quechua communities can also be found in Argentina, Brazil, and northern Chile.

Quechua Life and Culture Today

In the first years of the twenty-first century, the Quechua still lead predominantly agricultural lives. They tend to form tight-knit communities, with a strong sense of neighborliness holding each community together. Constructing a house, for example, is a communal activity in which several families come together to contribute time and labor toward completing the task. In return, the family whose house is being built not only provides food and beverages to those who are helping them, but also promises to help in the future those who have helped them.

Quechua society is generally male-centered. Positions of power in the community are usually filled by men, but within the home, women possess considerable influence. Children are an important part of Quechua family life, and male babies are generally favored over female ones. Many Quechua families have three or four children, but some families are known to have ten or more children. Most Quechua children do not receive much formal education because their contributions of labor in the fields are considered more important than attending school.

Potatoes were first cultivated in Peru around 2500 B.C. Since then, potatoes have become a major staple in the Quechua diet and are commonly eaten with spicy stews of meat and vegetables. Roasted or grilled guinea pigs are a Quechua delicacy.

Opposite: A Bolivian woman, wearing a hat and shawl in a style that is characteristic of the Quechua, smiles while looking away from the camera. The Quechua were banned from wearing their traditional clothes during Spanish colonial rule. Since then, Quechua women have worn Western-style skirts and blouses with woven shawls wrapped around their shoulders, while Quechua men wear ponchos over their shirts and trousers. Both Quechua men and women favor wearing sandals.

Silver Mines of Potosí

Located about 56 miles (90 km) southwest of Sucre and at an altitude of 13,290 feet (4,050 km), Potosí is famous for being one of the world's highest cities. Founded in the sixteenth century, the city of Potosí has a rich and historic beginning. Nearby Potosí Mountain was the location of legendary silver mines that brought great wealth to the Spanish Empire between the 1500s and 1600s.

The Road to Colonial Splendor

In the mid-1540s, Diego Huallpa, an Amerindian, became the first person to find silver ore in the Potosí region. News of his discovery spread quickly, and within a year, the city of Potosí was founded at the foothill of Potosí Mountain. The tremendous amount of silver ore that was later mined from Potosí Mountain led locals to nickname it "Cerro Rico," which means "Rich Hill." In thirty years, Potosí's population rose to 120,000, making it the largest city in the New World at that time. Potosí's population peaked at 160,000 in 1650. By then, silver from the Potosí mines had made Spain one of the world's richest nations.

Left: Bolivian miners working in or near the Potosí mines today endure appalling working conditions that are minimally different from those faced by their predecessors centuries ago.

At the height of Potosí's prosperity, wealthy Spanish families built lavish homes and richly decorated, Baroque-style churches in the city. Many of these sixteenth- and seventeenth-century buildings, including the Casa de la Moneda, Church of San Lorenzo, and Convent of Santa Teresa, still stand in Potosí, lending the city a distinctive colonial charm. In 1987, the United Nations Educational, Scientific, and Cultural Organization (UNESCO) declared Potosí a World Heritage Site because of the city's historic beginnings and colonial architecture.

Above: **Miners working in the Potosí mines today mainly dig for tin. Smaller amounts of other metals, such as copper, lead, and zinc, also have been found. Occasionally, some silver is unearthed.**

From Silver to Tin

Potosí's woes began in the early 1700s, when an outbreak of disease wiped out much of the city's population. By the early 1800s, Potosí's silver mining industry had completely lost its sparkle. The mountain's reserves of silver were nearly depleted, and less than 20,000 people lived in the city. Later, in the 1800s, tin mining replaced silver mining as the main economic activity in Potosí, and the city experienced a second but significantly smaller wave of growth. By the twenty-first century, even tin had been depleted past the point of commercial profitability in the Potosí mines. Nevertheless, many Bolivians today, including young boys, continue to scrape the Potosí mines for tin and small amounts of other metals, such as copper, lead, and zinc.

Tiwanaku Civilization

The Tiwanaku Ruins

Located about 34 miles (55 km) south of Lake Titicaca and nearly 13,000 feet (3,962 m) above sea level, the ruins of Tiwanaku tell of an ancient civilization that dominated the Andean region in pre-Inca times. Although some scientists claim to have found remains at Tiwanaku that date back to as early as 200 B.C., most of the Tiwanaku ruins date back to between A.D. 200 and A.D. 600. Experts generally agree that Tiwanaku power and influence began expanding into present-day eastern Bolivia, northern Chile, and southern Peru around 1000. By 1200, however, the people of Tiwanaku had all mysteriously disappeared, and they left behind few traces apart from the ruins found in western Bolivia today.

Ancient Technologies

Archaeological evidence shows that the people of Tiwanaku were exceptional agriculturalists and architects. Tiwanaku's people were self-sufficient. They fished and herded llamas for meat and cultivated their staples, such as potatoes and quinoa. In order to overcome the harsh climatic conditions of the Altiplano, where crops such as potatoes and quinoa traditionally would not have thrived, the people of Tiwanaku devised a clever

Left: The walls of the Kalasasaya, a Tiwanaku temple, are decorated with carved stone heads. The Kalasasaya temple and the Akapana pyramid are two of the more important structures of the Tiwanaku ruins. Located to the south of the Kalasasaya temple, the Akapana is a stepped pyramid that measures about 56 feet (17 m) high and has a base area of about 656 square feet (61 square m). In 2000, the United Nations Educational, Scientific, and Cultural Organization (UNESCO) declared the Tiwanaku ruins in Bolivia a World Heritage Site.

farming and irrigation system, known today as raised-field agriculture. Tiwanaku farmers first dug canals into the ground, with the distances between canals ranging from 16 to 30 feet (5 and 9 m). The soil that had been dug up was then piled in the areas between the canals to create raised plant beds. The canals later served not only to irrigate the crops, but also to trap heat from the sun. Heated canals prevented the crops from freezing overnight. Aquatic plants and algae grew in the canals, and Tiwanaku farmers used this organic matter from the canals to fertilize their cultivated crops.

Tiwanaku architecture has captured the imagination of many scientists, archaeologists, and observers, both past and present. No one has been able to explain how the Tiwanaku builders achieved the remarkable precision they did with the limited tools they had. Tiwanaku builders used cut stones in their construction, and many were monoliths, or massive pieces of stone that weighed an estimated 100 tons (91 tonnes) each. Experts today remain baffled by how the Tiwanaku builders moved the stones, squared them so perfectly, and fitted them together without a sealing agent such as mortar or plaster.

Above: **A large monolithic sculpture stands at the entrance of the Kalasasaya temple. The stones Tiwanaku builders used were usually made of either sandstone or andesite, a black volcanic rock.**

Uyuni Salt Flat

Located in southwestern Bolivia, Salar De Uyuni, or the Uyuni Salt Flat, is a vast, salt-covered wasteland measuring about 4,085 square miles (10,582 square km). Dominating the southern and lowest part of the Altiplano, the Uyuni Salt Flat is 11,995 feet (3,656 m) above sea level and is the largest salt flat in Bolivia. Called the Coipasa Salt Flat, the second-largest salt flat in the country lies not far to the north and is separated from the Uyuni Salt Flat by a series of hills.

A Harsh and Marvelous Landscape

At once forbidding and captivating, the landscape of the Uyuni Salt Flat changes with the seasons. In summer, frequent showers turn the salt flat into a large, shallow lake, with average depths ranging from 24 to 31 inches (60 to 80 cm). In winter, the lake dries up and leaves behind a thick layer of snow-white salt.

To this day, no one is certain how the Uyuni Salt Flat formed. Some experts have speculated that the salt flat came to exist because large amounts of salty mineral residue washed down from the mountains and accumulated over time on the Altiplano's flat surface. Other experts have suggested that the salt flat is what is left of a massive prehistoric lake that once covered most of southwestern Bolivia.

Below: **A salt pool has been built near the Hotel Playa Blanca, the only hotel located at the Uyuni Salt Flat. Also known as Salt Palace and Spa, Hotel Playa Blanca is unique because it was built entirely from salt blocks, from its foundation to its walls to the tables and chairs inside.**

The Town of Uyuni

Located to the east of the Uyuni Salt Flat, the town of Uyuni rests at an altitude of 12,024 feet (3,665 m) above sea level. Founded in 1890, the town of Uyuni was once an important railway junction and a prosperous mining and market center. Located to the northeast of the town are the Pulacayo and Huanchaca silver mines. Slav and Syrian colonists controlled the town's early economy. Serving as a stop on the country's main north-south railway line, the town of Uyuni was linked not only to other parts of Bolivia, but also, more importantly, to port facilities in Antofagasta in Chile.

Tourism

In recent years, the bizarre and beautiful landscape of the Uyuni Salt Flat has become a major tourist attraction. Adding to the magnificence of the vast natural formation is Isla de Pescadores, or Fisherman's Island, which is located in the middle of the salt flat and covered with giant cacti that sometimes reach 30 feet (9 m) in height. A population of viscachas, which are relatives of the chinchilla, also thrive on the island.

Above: **The sprawling Uyuni Salt Flat covers thousands of square miles on the Altiplano, and the climate there is typically cold and dry. Today, saltworks, such as Salinas de Garci Mendoza, Llica, and Calcha, surround the Uyuni Salt Flat and exploit the region's abundant natural resource to produce table salt.**

RELATIONS WITH NORTH AMERICA

The friendly and cooperative relations between Bolivia and the United States center on increasing trade and commerce between the two countries, assisting social and economic development in Bolivia, strengthening Bolivia's democratic institutions, and eliminating the illegal cultivation of coca plants in the country. Many U.S. businesses have subsidiaries in Bolivia, and U.S. direct investment in the country amounted to U.S. $2.1 billion at the end of 2002. This figure represents about 37.1 percent of the total direct foreign investment in Bolivia, making the United States the single largest foreign investor in the country.

Opposite: **A billboard on a street stall in a Cochabamba square advertises the U.S. soft drink giant Coca-Cola.**

Cultural exchanges between the people of Bolivia and North America take place through volunteer, research, and development programs, as well as through visits by musicians between the two regions. Bolivia is also a tourist destination for many North Americans who enjoy mountaineering in the Andes.

The Bolivian community in the United States is proud of its rich heritage. Several U.S.-based Bolivian folk-dancing troupes give Americans the opportunity to sample Bolivian culture. Bolivian restaurants in New York, California, Washington, and Ohio also show the Bolivian presence in the United States.

Above: **Volunteers from the U.S. Peace Corps work with Bolivians to repair a stone wall in the Andes countryside.**

Historical Ties

Historical records of the U.S. Department of State dating from the nineteenth and early twentieth centuries show a steady flow of contact between Bolivia and the United States. These contacts take the form of dispatches from U.S. ambassadors to Bolivia and from U.S. consuls based in La Paz to the United States. The U.S. Department of State has also kept a record of the internal political situation in Bolivia, as well as notes relating to Bolivia's relations with other countries. These valuable historical documents span the period between 1836 and 1929.

Diplomatic ties between Bolivia and the United States existed in the nineteenth century. The two countries made a treaty called the Treaty of Peace, Friendship, Commerce, and Navigation that was signed in La Paz on May 13, 1858, and ratified by both countries by 1862. Another treaty signed by Bolivia and the United States was the Extradition Convention of 1900, which allowed the extradition of fugitives between the two countries.

In 1880, during the War of the Pacific (1879–1883), the United States attempted to mediate between Chile, Bolivia, and Peru, but failed. These South American countries asked for U.S. assistance

Below: **Former Bolivian president Jorge Quiroga Ramírez shakes hands with U.S. president George W. Bush during an official visit to the White House on December 6, 2001.**

Left: **Former Bolivian first lady Yolanda Prada de Bánzer presented former U.S. secretary of state Madeleine Albright with a gift during the latter's visit to La Paz on August 18, 2000, during an official tour of South America.**

and intervention several times during the course of the war, and the United States played an important diplomatic role in helping to bring about peace.

The United States also helped mediate in the Chaco conflict that lasted from 1932 to 1935. During this time, Bolivia and Paraguay were at war. In 1938, a peace treaty was signed at a conference attended by delegates from Bolivia, Paraguay, other South American countries, and the United States.

A Difficult Time

The United States began offering development assistance to Bolivia in the 1940s. During World War II, Bolivia became an important source of tin for the United States.

Relations between the two countries grew tense, however, when a series of military governments came to power in Bolivia in the 1960s and 1970s. In 1971, the Bolivian government expelled U.S. Peace Corps volunteers from Bolivia. From the 1970s to the mid-1980s, the U.S. government suspected the Bolivian military government of having ties with drug traffickers. United States presidents Jimmy Carter and Ronald Reagan, therefore, refused to recognize Bolivia's military leadership. In June 1980, the Bolivian military expelled the U.S. ambassador from Bolivia. From July 1980 to November 1981, relations between Bolivia and the United States were officially suspended.

New Challenges

Current relations between the United States and Bolivia are friendly and cooperative, and the governments of both countries are committed to defending democracy, fighting terrorism, promoting economic growth, and battling drug trafficking.

The major challenge to relations between Bolivia and the United States is the issue of coca production in Bolivia. The coca plant has been grown in Bolivia for centuries, and Bolivians have been using the plant for various medicinal purposes. The leaves of the coca plant, however, form the basic ingredient in the illegal drug cocaine. Bolivian farmers do not take part in the actual production of cocaine, but their coca crops can be used to produce the drug. Cocaine use has harmful effects, and the U.S. government is working closely with the Bolivian government to reduce the production of coca in Bolivia.

Much U.S. financial aid to Bolivia goes toward encouraging farmers to plant crops other than coca. In this way, Bolivia has managed to reduce illegal coca plantations by more than 90 percent. However, Bolivian farmers have staged strong protests against the U.S. and Bolivian governments for taking away their main source of income. The farmers argue that their earnings from the sale of other crops is not enough to cover their basic expenses.

Left: **Former U.S. secretary of the treasury Laurence Summers (***left***) signs a debt relief agreement as Bolivia's former minister of finance Herbert Muller (***right***) looks on. Under this agreement, signed on December 2, 1999, in Santa Cruz, the United States canceled Bolivian debts of U.S. $12.3 million.**

Left: Bolivian minister of foreign affairs and worship Carlos Saavedra Bruno (*right*) greets U.S. assistant secretary of state for the Bureau of Western Hemisphere Affairs Otto Reich (*left*) during the latter's visit to La Paz in October 2002.

Economic Relations

The United States enjoys close economic and commercial relations with Bolivia. In 2002, U.S. exports to Bolivia totaled U.S. $283 million, while Bolivia's exports to the United States amounted to U.S. $162 million. Bolivia's main exports to the United States are gold, jewelry, tin, and wood products. Bolivia imports computers, machinery, vehicles, and wheat from the United States.

Commercial and economic treaties between Bolivia and the United States help promote trade and commerce between the two countries. The 2001 U.S.-Bolivian Bilateral Investment Treaty helps guarantee the rights of U.S. investors in Bolivia. The Andean Trade Promotion and Drug Eradication Act passed by the United States in 2002 also strengthens economic ties with Bolivia. This act renews and expands the Andean Trade Preference Act of 1991, which allows Andean countries, such as Bolivia, access to the U.S. market without having to pay customs duties. These initiatives are further strengthened by the U.S. government's Andean Regional Initiative, which is an aid package for Andean countries that promotes law enforcement, security, and social and economic development and improves judicial systems and antidrug campaigns.

Peace Corps Volunteers in Bolivia

Begun in 1962, the U.S. Peace Corps program in Bolivia was suspended in 1971. It resumed nearly twenty years later, in 1990. More than two thousand U.S. volunteers have lived and worked in Bolivia under the Peace Corps program. In 2002, about 150 U.S. volunteers engaged in development work in Bolivia, assisting on projects in areas such as agriculture, environmental management, water and sanitation, and community tourism development. Agricultural volunteers teach farmers to conserve soil, while other volunteers work with local communities to improve Bolivia's environment. Volunteers working in community tourism help Bolivians plan tourism projects that are both profitable and environmentally and culturally sustainable. Water sanitation volunteers help build and maintain potable water systems in rural communities and teach Bolivians better water management techniques.

Peace Corps volunteers who have returned to the United States have established *Amigos de Bolivia y Peru* in New Mexico. This group organizes activities that help members stay in touch with each other as well as with issues relating to Bolivia and Peru.

Above: **American music director David Handel, current music director of the National Symphony Orchestra of Bolivia, leads the group's first outdoor performance at the Uyuni Salt Flat in October 2001. Handel has been the Bolivian National Symphony Orchestra's music director since 1997.**

USAID in Bolivia

The United States is one of the two largest bilateral donors in Bolivia. The United States Agency for International Development (USAID) is a major U.S. aid agency that has been working in Bolivia to improve the country's social and economic conditions. Projects initiated by USAID in Bolivia fall under six broad categories: improving the Bolivian legal system by reducing delays in the administration of justice; developing business and trade in rural areas; improving health care and medical services; managing Bolivia's rich environmental resources in a sustainable manner; promoting alternative crops for coca farmers; and strengthening democratic institutions and those that promote conflict resolution. To support these objectives, USAID has requested over U.S. $97 million in the 2004 fiscal year.

The agency also supports development work carried out by U.S. charitable organizations in Bolivia. These groups include Save the Children and the International Eye Foundation, both of which work to improve the lives of children living in rural areas. U.S. nongovernmental organizations can receive grants from USAID for development work undertaken in Bolivia. USAID also funds teacher-training and adult-literacy programs in Bolivia.

Below: **A group of tourists from the United States visits the ancient ruins of Tiwanaku.**

American Presence in Bolivia

The U.S. embassy in Bolivia estimates that there are between seventeen and twenty thousand U.S. citizens living in Bolivia. Some U.S. businesses that have a presence in Bolivia include Nortel Networks, a telecommunications company, and NGR Energy. Other U.S. enterprises that operate within Bolivia's energy sector include Duke Energy International and Tenaska. In Bolivia's transportation sector, the railway line connecting Santa Cruz with Brazil and Argentina is managed by U.S.-based company Genessee & Wyoming.

American researchers visit Bolivia to carry out various studies and research projects. The U.S.-based Fulbright Program offers U.S. students the opportunity to come to Bolivia for one academic year to carry out independent research. In 2003, Fulbright grants were handed out to four U.S. students to undertake research in Bolivia. Other U.S. researchers working in Bolivia include faculty members from universities. Staff from the University of Pennsylvania Museum, for example, have been carrying out archaeological research in the Bolivian Amazon, while researchers from the University of California, Los Angeles have excavated in the Lake Titicaca basin.

Below: **Azul Azul, a popular Bolivian musical group that mixes folk music and pop tunes, joins a Mexican band to celebrate the Fiesta Broadway, a Latin festival in Los Angeles, in April 2001.**

Below: **Members of Bolivian musical group Azul Azul pose for the cameras in Los Angeles in April 2001.**

Bolivians in the United States

The state of Virginia has a strong Bolivian community and is the home of Sangre Boliviana, a Bolivian folk dancing troupe. Founded in 1987, the group promotes traditional Bolivian folk music and dancing. The group has performed at many state and national events, including the National Cherry Blossom Festival Parade and the Festival Latino. Renacer Boliviano is another Bolivian-American cultural group that promotes Bolivian traditions and customs in the United States. Based in the Chicago area, Renacer Boliviano organizes performances and festivals of Bolivian folk dances and music. The organization is also a charitable foundation, with the aim of helping underprivileged children in Bolivia. The New York-based Quipus Bolivia Cultural Council and the North Carolina-Cochabamba Partners of the Americas are other organizations that promote Bolivian culture in the United States and fund development projects in Bolivia.

The United States is home to some prominent Bolivian-born residents, including educator Jaime Escalante and violinist and conductor Jaime Laredo. Cochabamba-born Jaime Laredo has had an impressive forty-year career as a violinist and conductor, performing with more than one hundred orchestras across the United States as well as internationally. He has recorded over forty compact discs of music and won a Grammy Award in 1991 in the category of Best Chamber Music Performance, an award he shared with musicians Emanuel Ax, Isaac Stern, and Yo-Yo Ma.

Left: **Actor Edward James Olmos plays inspiring Bolivian teacher Jaime Escalante in the film** *Stand and Deliver.* **The movie depicted Escalante's real-life efforts in teaching and encouraging poor Latino students to take and pass an Advanced Placement calculus test.**

Jaime Escalante

The story of mathematics, physics, and computer teacher Jaime Escalante is one of the most inspiring immigrant success stories in the United States. The son of two teachers, Escalante was born in La Paz. He taught physics and mathematics in his home country for more than ten years before immigrating to the United States with his family in 1964. At first, Escalante could not speak English and did not possess the credentials that he needed to find a job as a teacher. Instead of settling for a low-paying job, Escalante enrolled in night classes at a community college while working during the day. After earning both a degree in electronics and his teaching credentials from California State University, Los Angeles, Escalante began teaching math at Garfield High School, located in a rough section of East Los Angeles, in 1976. The movie *Stand and Deliver* (1988) tells the story of his efforts to help disadvantaged Latino students. Escalante has received many awards, including the Presidential Medal for Excellence in 1998. He is the host of *Futures With Jaime Escalante*, an award-winning science and math television series.

Bolivia's Relations With Canada

Diplomatic relations between Bolivia and Canada are cordial. In 1999, Canadian secretary of state for Latin America and Africa David Kilgour visited Bolivia and met with then Bolivian foreign minister Javier Murillo de la Rocha. January 2000 marked the first visit to Bolivia by a Canadian foreign minister. A Canadian consulate was established in Bolivia later that year. In June 2002, Canadian officials observed Bolivia's national elections and reported that the elections were free, fair, and peaceful. A year later, Canada's minister for international cooperation, Susan Whelan, visited Bolivia.

Canada has been involved in development projects in Bolivia since 1969. The Canadian government's international aid agency, Agence Canadienne de Développement International (CIDA), funded projects in Bolivia costing CAN $23.1 million in 2001. In Bolivia, CIDA promotes development in various areas, including health care and water sanitation. In health care, CIDA works with the Bolivian government to improve the public health system in Bolivia. Building water sanitation systems in poor rural areas of Bolivia is another objective of CIDA's assistance program in the country.

Left: **A Canadian volunteer works in Inti Wara Yassi, an animal refuge in Villa Tunari.**

BOLIVIA

Country Boundary
State Boundary
■ **Capital**
● **City**
◆ **Historical Site**
〜 **River**

A   B   C   D

1

PANDO

B R A Z I L

N

2

PERU

Mamoré

Beni

Lake
Rogoaguado

**NOEL KEMPFF
MERCADO
NATIONAL PARK**

**MADIDI
NAT'L
PARK**

Lake
Rogagua

Iténez

B E N I

Huiñaymarca

LA PAZ

Lake Chucuito

Condoriri
(18,530 ft /
5,648m)

Isla del Sol

Lake
Titicaca

Isla de la Luna

Huayna Potosí
(19,975 ft /
6,088m)

3

Copacabana

Coripata

Concepción

El Alto   **LA PAZ**

Strait of Tiquina

Tiwanaku   Illimani
(20,741 ft / 6,322 m to
21,201 ft / 6,462 m)

Villa Tunari

SANTA CRUZ

Copacabana
Peninsula

Patacamaya

Desaguadero

Cochabamba

Sajama
National
Park

COCHABAMBA

Oruro

Santa
Cruz

Arica

Sajama
(21,463 ft / 6,542 m)

**AMBORÓ
NATIONAL
PARK**

ORURO

Lake
Poopó

Coipasa

Cal Orcko

Yacuces

Fisherman's
Island

Coipasa
Salt Flat

Betanzos

SUCRE

Tarabuco

4

Uyuni
Salt Flat

Potosí

PACIFIC OCEAN

Cerro Rico

CHUQUISACA

Chaco Boreal

Uyuni

POTOSÍ

Tarija

CHILE

Pilcomayo

TARIJA

PARAGUAY

5

Antofagasta

ARGENTINA

Tropic of Capricorn

86

Above: Locals wear colorful costumes during celebrations for the Festival of the Virgin in Copacabana.

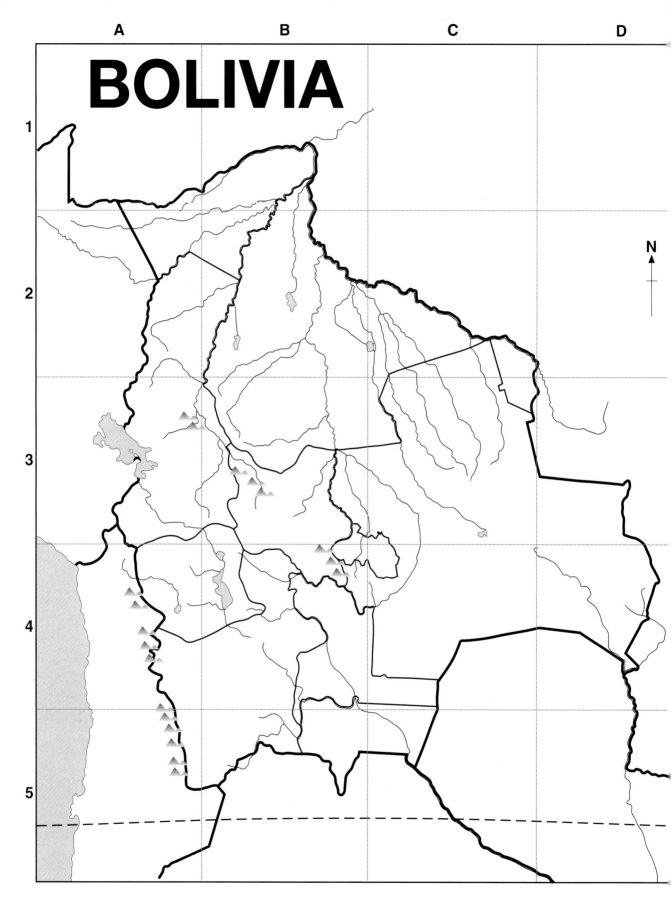

BOLIVIA

N

Above: The snow-covered summit of Huayna Potosí looks stunning against the deep-blue Bolivian sky.

How Is Your Geography?

Learning to identify the main geographical areas and points of a country can be challenging. Although it may seem difficult at first to memorize the locations and spellings of major cities or the names of mountain ranges, rivers, deserts, lakes, and other prominent physical features, the end result of this effort can be very rewarding. Places you previously did not know existed will suddenly come to life when referred to in world news, whether in newspapers, television reports, other books and reference sources, or on the Internet. This knowledge will make you feel a bit closer to the rest of the world, with its fascinating variety of cultures and physical geography.

This map can be duplicated for use in a classroom. (PLEASE DO NOT WRITE IN THIS BOOK!) Students can then fill in any requested information on their individual map copies. The student can also make a copy of the map and use it as a study tool to practice identifying place names and geographical features on his or her own.

Bolivia at a Glance

Official Name   República de Bolivia (Republic of Bolivia)

Capital   Sucre (legal capital; seat of the judiciary);
La Paz (administrative capital)

Official Languages   Aymara, Quechua, and Spanish

Population   8,445,134 (July 2002 estimate)

Land Area   424,164 square miles (1,098,580 square kilometers)

Departments   Beni, Chuquisaca, Cochabamba, La Paz, Oruro, Pando, Potosí, Santa Cruz, and Tarija

Border Countries   Brazil, Paraguay, Argentina, Chile, and Peru

Highest Point   Mount Sajama 21,463 feet (6,542 meters)

Lowest Point   Rio Paraguay 295 feet (90 meters)

Major Rivers   Beni, Desaguadero, Guaporé, Madre de Dios, Mamoré, Mauri, Pilcamayo, Río de la Plata, and Río Paraguay

Major Cities   Cochabamba, La Paz, Oruro, Potosí, Santa Cruz, Sucre, and Tarija

Head of Government   Gonzalo Sánchez de Lozada Bustamente (since August 4, 2002)

Famous Leaders   General Antonio Jóse de Sucre, Víctor Paz Estenssoro, General Hugo Bánzer Suárez

Major Religions   Roman Catholic, Protestant (Evangelical Methodist)

Holidays   New Year's Day (January 1); Good Friday (mid-April); Labor Day (May 1); Independence Day (August 6); Christmas (December 25)

Major Exports   Soybeans, natural gas, zinc, gold, and wood

Major Imports   Capital goods, raw materials and semimanufactures

Major Industries   Clothing, food and beverages, handicrafts, petroleum, smelting, tin mining, and tobacco

Currency   Boliviano 6.91 = U.S. $1 (since January 2002)

Opposite: **This sculpture guards the Kalasasaya Temple, the center of the ancient Tiwanaku civilization.**

Glossary

Bolivian Vocabulary

ají (ah-HEE): Bolivian hot chili peppers.

ají amarillo (ah-HEE ah-mah-REE-yoh): a type of pepper that is usually dried and powdered and used to season various Bolivian dishes.

cacho (KAH-choh): a dice game.

Ch'aque de Quinua (CHAH-kay day KEEN-wah): a Bolivian soup consisting of quinoa, potatoes, tomatoes, leeks, carrots, and broad beans.

charango (cha-RAHN-goh): a small guitar traditionally made from the empty shell of an armadillo.

charqui (CHAHR-kee): preserved meat.

Chupe de papaliza (CHOO-pay day pah-pah-LEE-zah): a Bolivian soup made from a yellow potato called *papaliza*, broad beans, and squash.

cueca (KWEH-kah): a Bolivian dance influenced by Spanish music.

diablada (dee-ah-BLAH-dah): a dance in which the performers wear masks that depict the faces of devils. The dance is usually performed during carnival time.

El Libertador (EHL lee-behr-tah-DOHR): the unofficial title given to Simón Bolívar, meaning "the liberator."

entrada (en-TRAH-dah): a colorful daylong procession of music and dance groups that takes place at festivals.

futbolín (foot-boh-LEAN): foosball.

gorros (GOH-rohs): colorful ear-flapped caps woven from llama wool.

huayño (WHY-nyo): an Amerindian form of music and dance.

locoto (loh-KOH-toe): a type of Bolivian chili pepper that is harvested when bright red in color; also called *rocoto.*

majao (ma-JOW): a dish of rice and meat that is served with fried plantain, egg, and cassava.

morenada (more-ren-NAH-dah): a colorful and lively dance performed at carnival celebrations in Oruro.

mita (MEE-tah): a system of forced labor instituted by the Spanish colonial rulers.

paceños (pah-SEH-neos): people from La Paz.

polleras (poh-YAY-rahs): full skirts worn by Aymara women.

quena (KEH-nah): Andean flute.

quirquiña (keer-KEEN-nya): a Bolivian herb that is frequently used in salads and salsa sauces.

salteñas (sahl-TEHN-nahs): meat turnovers.

sapo (SAH-poh): a game in which players score points by throwing tokens into the mouth of a metal toad; literally means "toad."

Semana Santa (seh-MAH-nah SAHN-tah): the Christian celebration of Holy Week.

siku (SEE-koo): Andean panpipes.

sikuri (see-KOOH-ree): a type of Bolivian dance, as well as the name for the music performed by a group of siku players.

tarka (TAHR-kah): a soft-sounding Bolivian wind instrument.

Todos Santos (TOE-dose SAHN-tose): called All Saints' Day in English, a Bolivian festival celebrated in November that honors the souls of the dead.

trompos (TROHM-pohs): tops.

ulupica (ooh-loo-PEE-kah): a type of chili pepper that grows wild in Bolivia and Peru.

viernes de soltero (bee-EHR-nehs deh sol-TEH-roh): a Friday night gathering at a local bar.

English Vocabulary

abstract: art that has little or no resemblence to recognizable objects is described as being abstract.

adobe: sun-dried brick made of clay and straw; a building constructed from these bricks is also called an adobe.

alabaster: a smooth white or translucent type of gypsum that is often carved into vases and other ornaments.

alloy: a substance that is a mixture of two or more metals.

Amerindians: indigenous people native to the Americas.

Altiplano: the flat plain located in the Andes Mountains, where a significant proportion of Bolivia's population lives.

archaeologists: scientists who study the material remains (fossil relics, artifacts, and monuments) of past human life and activities.

basalt: a hard, dark gray or black rock that can be carved into sculptures.

bipedal: having two feet.

coup: the sudden takeover of a government by using force or violence.

depleted: reduced in quantity to the point of disappearing altogether.

dispute: a quarrel.

enthusiasts: people who are deeply committed to an activity or cause.

ethnobotany: the study of the knowledge accumulated by a certain ethnic group about the plants and trees around them and how this group views and uses plants in their daily lives.

fusion: a combination of different styles.

glacier: a large body of ice moving slowly down a slope or valley or spreading outward on a land surface.

holistic: relating to complete systems rather than parts.

massif: the part of a mountain range that contains several summits in a compact area.

monolith: a large piece of stone; a tall statue or sculpture made from one single piece of stone.

onyx: a hard translucent mineral that comes in many colors and can be used for sculpturing.

ponchos: blankets with slits in the middle that can be slipped over the head and worn as sleeveless garments.

porter: a person who assists mountain climbers by carrying their equipment, food, and other supplies.

pre-Columbian: pertaining to the Americas before the arrival of Columbus.

privatized: transferred control of a public or government company to a private corporation.

quinoa: a nutritious grain indigenous to the Andes.

staples: basic food items that are eaten daily and form an important part of one's diet.

Yungas: a group of fertile valleys in the Amazon Basin of Bolivia.

More Books to Read

Airplane Boys with the Revolutionists in Bolivia. Airplane Boys series.
E. J. Crane, E. J. Craine (Purdue University Press)

The Aymara of South America. First Peoples series. James Eagen
(Lerner Publications)

Bolivia. Cultures of the World series. Robert Pateman (Benchmark)

Bolivia. Enchantment of the World second series. Byron Augustin
(Children's Book Press)

Bolivia. Major World Nations series. Karen Schimmel (Chelsea House)

Bolivia. Discovering South America series. LeeAnne Gelletly
(Mason Crest Publishers)

Bolivia in Pictures. Visual Geography series. Mary M. Rodgers, editor (Lerner)

Ecuador Peru Bolivia. Country Fact Files series. Edward Parker (Raintree)

Simon Bolivar: South American Liberator. Hispanic Biographies series.
David Goodnough (Enslow)

Videos

Globe Trekker: Bolivia. (555 Productions)

Full Circle with Michael Palin: Chile/Bolivia and Peru. (PBS Home Video)

Climbing Bolivia's Huayna Potosí Part 1 & 2. (Wellspring Media, Inc.)

Web Sites

www.boliviaweb.com

www.bolivia.start4all.com

www.ddg.com/LIS/aurelia/bolivi.htm

www.odci.gov/cia/publications/factbook/geos.bl.html

Due to the dynamic nature of the Internet, some web sites stay current longer than others. To find additional web sites, use a reliable search engine with one or more of the following keywords to help you locate information about Bolivia. Keywords: *Altiplano, Aymara, Simón Bolívar, La Paz, mestizo baroque, Quechua, Santa Cruz, Tiwanaku.*

Index

95